SOM CERTAINE SONETS

Borgo Press Books by Michael R. Collings

All Calm, All Bright: Christmas Offerings
The Art and Craft of Poetry: Twenty Exercises Toward Mastery
Brian Aldiss
Dark Transformations: Deadly Visions of Change
Devil's Plague: A Mystery Novel
The Films of Stephen King
GemLore: An Introduction to Precious and Semi-Precious Gemstones
The House Beyond the Hill: A Novel of Horror
In Endless Morn of Light: Moral Freedom in Milton's Universe
In the Void: Poems of Science Fiction, Myth and Fantasy, & Horror
The Many Facets of Stephen King
Matrix: Echoes of Growing Up West
Naked to the Sun: Dark Visions of Apocalypse
The Nephiad: An Epic Poem in XII Books
Piers Anthony
Scaring Us to Death: The Impact of Stephen King on Popular Culture
Singer of Lies: A Science Fantasy Novel
The Slab: A Novel of Horror
Som Certaine Sonets, Revised and Enlarged Edition
Tales Through Time: Poems, Revised and Enlarged Edition
Three Tales of Omne: A Companion to Wordsmith
Toward Other Worlds: Perspectives on John Milton, C. S. Lewis, Stephen King, Orson Scott Card, and Others
Wer *Means* Man, *and Other Tales of Wonder and Terror*
Wordsmith, Part One: The Veil of Heaven
Wordsmith, Part Two: The Thousand Eyes of Flame

SOM CERTAINE SONETS

REVISED AND ENLARGED EDITION

MICHAEL R. COLLINGS

THE BORGO PRESS
MMXI

SOM CERTAINE SONETS

Copyright © 1996, 1998, 1999, 2002, 2011 by
Michael R. Collings

FIRST BORGO PRESS EDITION

Published by Wildside Press LLC

www.wildsidebooks.com

DEDICATION

For Judi,

Whose presence lives in them all,

and

For Rob,

Who shared the pains
Of bringing this book—
And its older siblings—
To fruition

CONTENTS

INTRODUCTION 9

EPYLLION IN ANAMNESIS 15

ELEMENTAL SONETS 85

A BANQUET OF SONETS 123

MISCELLANY. 143

BIBLIOGRAPHY 153

TITLE INDEX 155

ABOUT THE AUTHOR 161

INTRODUCTION
WHY "SONETS"?

Sonnets are among the most widely recognized of poetic forms. They enjoy a long tradition, dating back almost a thousand years; in English, they first became widely popular some four and a half centuries ago and have retained that popularity ever since. They have been written by the great, the near-great, and the I-wish-I-were-great. Sidney, Spenser, Shakespeare, Milton, Wordsworth, Meredith, Robinson—all and more explored the possibilities of sonnets.

In general, we think we can easily understand what a sonnet is. It has fourteen lines, with ten syllables per line (often giving it a highly recognizable box-like shape). It has a distinct rhythm: five stressed syllables per line, alternating with five unstressed syllables. It has a distinct rhyme pattern—or rather, it may choose from one of several distinct rhyme patterns, the most common generally labeled Italian/Petrarchan, English/Shakespearean, or Spenserian. It has a recognizable structure—in English, three sets of four lines followed by a set of two, each of the sets frequently separated by white space. It has a consistent tone: usually serious, philosophical, meditative, political; at times rhapsodic, ecstatic, spiritual. In other words, the sonnet can be a little bit of everything.

Of course, along with this kind of genre recognition, along with its long heritage and superficially commonplace structure, come distinct challenges for the sonnet writer:

- The sonnet is old fashioned;
- The sonnet frequently sounds archaic;
- The sonnet is self-consciously poetic;
- The sonnet allows no variation or exploration;
- The sonnet is, to many modern tastes, *passé*.

A glance at the entry under "sonnet" in *The New Princeton Encyclopedia of Poetry and Poetics,* however, immediately disabuses one of many of these preconceptions. Sonnets remain a vital part of contemporary literature. They are capable of infinite variations of form, structure, tone, and content. They appeal to writers of all levels and all interests. And they appear in a stunning variety of forms: free-verse sonnets, blank-verse sonnets, word-count sonnets, slant-rhyme sonnets, 12-line sonnets, 16-line sonnets, 18-line sonnets, and on and on.

While this abundance may strike readers as bordering on chaos, the versatility and variety of the contemporary sonnet actually reflects the origins of the name by which we conventionally call the form. John Donne's collection of poetry, which appeared in the seventeenth-century under the title *Songs and Sonets*, provides an excellent case in point.

Sonets, not *sonnets*.

'Little songs'—lyrics that sometimes but not always appeared in a comparatively rigid format but that could also take on a bewildering variety of shapes.

As soon as the spelling regularized/conventionalized to 'sonnets,' however, lithification set in. So many lines. So many syllables per line. Such and such a rhyme scheme. Thus and so for structure.

Som Certaine Sonets attempts to regain the original sense of experimentation, of versatility, of possibility that characterized poems such as Donne's. There are *sonnets* here—strict exercises in predetermined form and structure. But there are also *sonets*—lyrics that suggest fourteen lines of iambic pentameter rather than reproduce them. Many of the sonets are syllabic, with either nine or eleven syllables per line but no attempt at consistent meter. Some seek to recapitulate the rhythms of colloquial speech rather than those of formal verse. Many use slant rhyme, and particularly assonance, to connect lines, rather than strict masculine rhyme. Many consciously blur the distinction between quatrains, forcing grammatical units to leap white space, or, alternatively, fracturing neat couplets by breaking bits of lines away from one and assigning them to another. Some depend for their effect on words that are not there, with blanks and white space functioning as essential components to meaning; others attempt to give the readers everything needed to understand and appreciate.

Som Certaine Sonets represents poetry written over a forty-year span, 1969-2009. While the poems do not appear in order of composition, they fall logically into several sequences:

- *EPYLLION IN ANAMNESIS* consisting of:

    REMEMBERY, first published as two sequences, appeared as issues of the Internet online journal, *Ygdrasil* (1996 and 1998);

    TALIESIN, first published with *Remembery I* as *Epyllion in Anamnesis,* focuses on mythic, religious, and symbolic patterns in combining Arthurian motifs with the history of Joseph Smith and the founding of the Church of Jesus Christ of Latter-day Saints;

- *ELEMENTAL SONETS*, first published as the July 1999 issue of *Ygdrasil*; subsequently augmented and reprinted as *Elementals: Auto-Reductive Sonets in Major and Minor Modes* (Zarahemla Motets, July 1999), expanded to include inter-cut quotations from John A. Widtsoe, Parley P. Pratt, and others;

- *A BANQUET OF SONETS*, first published as an issue of the Internet online journal, *Ygdrasil* (May 2002), partly suggested by "Ovid's Banquet of the Senses" by the Renaissance poet George Chapman; and

- *MISCELLANY,* following the practice of sixteenth-century editors in assembling a number of sonets unified by the simple fact of their form (or denial of the form, or variations on the form, or…well, enough said about that).

Within each segment some of the poems have been positioned with an eye to context, to themes, to forms; others appear in precisely that place in the sequence because…well, because that's where they seemed to fit best. For this collection, new poems have been added to each of the major divisions.

Within these guidelines—as flexible as they might be—I have attempted to remain true to the essence of the *sonet*. And I hope that in the process I have created some pieces that will be interesting, stimulating, and enjoyable.

Michael R. Collings
Meridian ID
January 2011

On Poetry as a Façade
Behind Which the Essence Lurks

Meter comes easily. English tends to
Shift and swirl in rhythmic fall-then-rise.
Syllables allow themselves (almost) no
Hesitance. Sounds link in subtle ways
But can be tracked and traced across crisp lines,
Arrows drawn if needed to make clear
How "m" persists, or "l," what strengths it gains
By repetition. What remains to mar
The texture of a piece, to hinder
Transformation from mere craft to art
(If one can hope for such in fonder
Thoughts) is that oblique, intrinsic part,
That revelatory, quintessential goal:
The power and the passion and the soul.

On Stress

In olden days, the sonnet's lines were built
With care to make the reader rise and fall
While ambling through the splendid, gaudy gilt
Of words in rhythms that must never stall;

In strictest forms, each line was fit with care
Into a predetermined march of stress;
Down, up, down, up—they strode with polished flair,
Creating their own forward-moving press.

But now—ah now!—poets may feel more free,
May shift their stresses—lightly—if they please,
Until sound and meaning cogently agree,
And meter echoes form with pleasant ease.

Still, under all, the heart-beat throbs persist,
Incessant, too demanding to resist.

EPYLLION IN ANAMNESIS

Epyllion in Anamnesis

Why Epyllion in Anamnesis?

In its strictest sense, *anamnesis* means little more than 'recalling to memory' or 'recollection'—although the act of recollecting is in itself a remarkable achievement, limited in its fullness, perhaps, to a single species. A thirteenth-century rhetorician, Boncompagno da Signa, rhapsodized upon human memory by placing it in the context of an entire lifetime:

> Memory is a glorious and admirable gift of nature by which we recall past things, we embrace present things, and we contemplate future things through their likeness to past things.
> Recollection thus becomes a human analogue to eternity and infinity, allowing past, present, and future to co-exist simultaneously within the imagination.

In its implications, however, *anamnesis* suggests far more than simple recollection. In an author's note appended to one of the modern poems most frequently mentioned as a legitimate heir to the epic tradition of Homer, Virgil, and Milton—David Jones' *The Anathemata*—Jones expands upon the word as follows:

> Anamnesis. I take leave to remind the reader that this is a key-word in our deposits. The dictionary defines its general meaning as 'the recalling of things past'. But what is the nature of this particular recalling? I append the following quotation as being clear and to the point: 'It (anamnesis) is not quite easy to represent accurately in English, words like "remembrance" or "memorial" having for us a connotation of something *absent* which is only mentally recollected. But in the

scriptures of both the Old and New Testament *anamnesis* and the cognate verb have a sense of "recalling" or "re-presenting" before God an event in the past so that it becomes *here and now operative by its effects*'.

Jones argues persuasively that poetry is "a kind of anamnesis of, i.e., is an effective recalling of, something loved"; in the words of one of Jones's interpreters,

> Thus if the Mass be regarded as a total anamnesis, 'a recalling of all the dead', 'of all times and places', *The Anathemata* is a partial anamnesis, a recalling of those loved things which have gone to the making of the poet. Not merely as a private individual, of course, but as the product of his culture. As David Jones says, 'one is trying to make a shape out of the very things of which one is oneself made'.

Recalling loved things central "to the making of the poet."
Envisioning the poet as "the product of his culture."

These are two goals of *Epyllion in Anamnesis*. The first segment, *Remembery*, is private. It focuses on images and memories from my own past, in part to re-create a slice of American life in the late 1950s and early 1960s, in part to suggest some of the assumptions and presumptions children of that decade have carried with them into the present. To that extent, *Remembery* is a small, private epic, an *epyllion*, exploring the genesis of a particular mind, a particular imagination in a particular place. It explores as well variations on another small, private mode, the sonnet, transformed through syllable count and slant rhyme into a vehicle for the conversational tone that seemed appropriate for *Remembery.*

Taliesin, on the other hand, presents a small *public* epic, again using for the most part modified sonnets, to create a mythic recollection of an important element of my culture: the life of

Joseph Smith and the founding of the Church of Jesus Christ of Latter-day Saints. *Taliesin* is *not* a foray into history, however; it is a mythic imagining—a recollecting, if you will—of key episodes from Joseph Smith's life, overlaid by the Arthurian mythos. The result is a unique vision of history and myth that suggests both but that is ultimately neither.

I appreciate initial readings of and responses to several of the *Taliesin* poems by Orson Scott Card (the original Friar Orison), Lee Allred, and Gideon Burton; the willingness of *Ygdrasil* magazine to publish the majority of *Remembery* as an online issue; and, as ever, the patience of my family during the process of composition.[1]

---

1. Originally included as "Author's Afterword" to the first edition of *Epyllion in Anamnesis*

EPYLLION IN ANAMNESIS I:

Remembery

Sonnet

Something there is that doesn't like a sonnet,
That shrugs out of poetic soil like rocks
In Frost's spring-field to ridicule and mock,
Find excuse to heap abuse upon it;
Something there is that cannot quite condone it,
This exercise in tightly rigid, stock
Schemes—rhythm, rhyme, and meter—to unlock
Humanity, to *sine-qua-non* it.

Yet something there is also, something strange
That draws us through the sonnet back into
REMEMBERY. Perhaps it is no more
Than sheer nostalgia for old dreams to range
Beyond our own blood-coursings, searching blue-
Fringed sunsets for a half-forgotten shore.

Amnesia

Our Birth is not a Sleep or a Forgetting,
As Wordsworth said, but more...and less—not *Sleep*
But deep *unConsciousness* preluding
Dreams and Visions in the darkened Deep
We now transgress. Nor *Forgetting* (which
Implies *Remembery* in this mortal
State) but strict *Amnesia*—'not-Remembery'—
Extended through long, dark, and lonely years;
Amnesiac unConsciousness more clearly
Satisfies parameters of this earthly
Life—more so than mere sleep or merely

Forgetting. We do not know who, or why,
Or how, or when we became of Earth—
R<small>EMEMBERY</small> begins its painful Birth.

Before the Throwing

Before the throwing-outward-state ignites,
a moment prior—pearlous instant
blood-suffused   breath-caught   flesh-fire—

she gasps to penetrate
potentiality (demanding imperatrix)
wills the throwing-outward to respond;

magnet to a periscope beyond black seas
that strains half-blind and blooded
by a setting sun—it glares to ruin.

Mockingbird and nightingale and mourning
dove—mutated songs curve toward
the magnet of a bleeding severed tongue

and and and*OH*and cataclysmic throwing-outward—
potentiality makes real the flash-fire wound

In the Old House on the Farm

I've never seen the place where I was born,
Do not remember ever seeing it,
Though vague images of woodwork, brick, and stone
Persist. A *Maternity Home*, she called
It on the few times that I asked. She wouldn't
Volunteer. So I have appropriated
A new birthplace: logs hand-hewn, chipped gray grout,
Age-softened splinters bearding warped door jambs.

Inside: smells of cobwebs mingled with untouched
Dust and threat of spiders—two cast-off wicker
Funeral-baskets—an old crank telephone
That sputtered random sparks—a Maytag washer
Wringer-less, chipped and gray—a memory-maze
Still echoing my mother's new-born cries.

Birth

I imagine her on bleak October days,
November nights of leaf-mold dreams
Compressed in random, zigzag ice-fence waves
Of birth-pangs as she scuffs and weaves
Alone along cold corridors. Outside
Stars cut incisions, birthing flame
That spills quick liquid life across spare white
Fields. Inside, wet spots of pain
Whisper in a mottled map of flesh
That sleeps close by. Now hunched and wan
She shuffles down dark corridors, ashen
Memories—discarded—tread on
Hot-milk pressing nipples that now
Dream of snowy drifts and icy dew.

From the Porch [I]

From the porch, we watched, she says, school children
trudge rough-graveled roads (not paved, not yet—
our subdivision still too new), clutching
books and bags and Howdy-Doody lunch-kits—
waving as they passed, she and I, who would
remain at home until raw afternoon
returned empty kits, and books, and children wild
for play. Each morning we watched wave on
wave of children pass, she says, smiled and waved
until their last departing feet transgressed

the corner lawn and disappeared. We rose,
she says, and dusted off the concrete dust
and went inside, where she deferred her daily chores
until she'd dressed me for the day in male attire.

The Children's Merry-Go-Round

The children's merry-go-round in the park
pie-segments kaleidoscope   blood-flushed cheeks
screams cut joy through lightning air   poker-flick
of sunburned shoulders   T-shirts flaring sleek

flames in a whirlwind   blood scorching my back
running rivers beneath my thin waistband
Beneath the pain hot blood on my back black
bolts and black screwheads painted red   stark red

hand of pain severing breath from shocked lungs
head spinning   body spinning   soul spinning
child's shock-cry lurking beneath blood-bit tongue
soul spinning   body spinning   blood spinning

kaleidoscoping on the merry-go-
-round in the park   fresh blood and laughter flow

Stringing Buttons

Stringing buttons—hunched on the worn pine floor,
Its planks velvet smooth from half-century
Of hands scrubbing, polishing—musty air
Warm with subtle gossip, whispered words we

Youngsters ignored.... We strung buttons on hanks
Of time-greyed cotton-thread and squabbled for
Favorites: foil-backed glass; glossy jet, ink-
Black-deep; mock turquoise; hand-cut bone, smooth, clear—

While hour on hour grandmothers stitched staid quilts,
Wove intricate lines with white cotton strands
Through patterns pieced from scraps—old aprons, shirts
Sunday dresses faded and worn breath-thin;

Our cotton threads coiled in the button box—
We never cared that none had end-thread knots.

Bruce and the Cow

We've laughed about the shot for decades now—
Three-year-old Bruce perched on the dusty hood
Of Dad's black office-issued Buick—a cow,
Boss or Roany or old Brownie, meandered
Through sunset brambles toward the barn,
Bag swinging heavily above fluffed milkweed
Heads, horns polled, inadequate to harm—
Trundling her way to milking and sweet feed—

Passing Bruce by inches, shambling
Between granary and tool-shed, where Dad
Had parked the car, where Bruce clutched grimacing
His fear, face etched with sun-down tear-stained red….
We've laughed at that stark photograph of Bruce,
And silently breathed thanks it wasn't us.

Nellie, Outside the House, Jerome ID, 1935

I live close now, not two hours distant
From their Depression farm. Finally at home
After sixty years, to a persistent
Sense that draws me just outside Jerome,

Where Grandpa built a house of cast-off boards
With newsprint on the walls, and twig-wrought chairs;
Where Grandma raised seven with no rewards

But silence, loneliness, and others' cares.

In one old print, she stands alone in snow
Outside the door; her only society
A sheep, and one far-distant house. Although
Loving words, she lived in mute anxiety.

Her journal tells of eight harsh wintry weeks
Of no converse with any but her boys;
Of ice and snow and tears upon her cheeks,
Howling winds and storms the only noise.

Winter Woman! I may travel frozen years
Yet barely know the landscape of your fears.

Grampa Collings

Fifty years ago, he sat in his bleached
cane chair beneath box elders. He rarely
spoke—growled sometimes. Blue bib-overalls stretched
across his belly, gray-stubble-chinned, barely
awake (it seemed), he sat, flicking black flies
with his handmade swatter—white cotton string
stitching fringed inner tube to a bent-wire
frame. When we got too rambunctious, he'd swing
a leather razor strop he'd lettered fifty
years before: "YOU'D BETTER BE GOOD." We were.

But now—with blue-light Zappers, No-Pest sticky
strips, steel Radials, canvas chairs for leisure,
Bic disposables, how are we to stop
rambunctious children   and with no razor strops?

Grandmother Collings's Church-House in Jerome

Grandmother Collings' church-house in Jerome—
Angular, imposing, brittle, cold—
Harsh walls of rough-cut iron-gray stone
Swallowed light. One window soared, winter-gold....

That's all I remember, fifty years
Long since—no words, no music from organ
Or choir, no hidden rustle as chairs
Shifted. Nothing but one dark wall-span,
One translucent window vault...and tiny
Glass communion cups nestled in long
Silver trays—glass so thin, so clarified
It seemed one brash thoughtless breath, one wrong-
Ways glance could shatter it...pierce my palm
With blessèd water that else would be balm.

Beyond the Plains

Inside the lid of my grandfather's coffin stood
an oak—leafless, gaunt—etched on pale
satin, icon for age-battered wood
surviving decade-storms of sleet and gale;
it matched his heart, his life-long quest for good,
his strength enfleshed to till the earth, prevail
against all foes in toilsome adulthood.

It speaks to me, that solitary tree,
that warder of his resting last remains,
reminding me that I still tread the deep-
scored trail dividing living grain, still see,
though distantly, the mount above flat plains
that beckons irresistibly to sleep.

In Elba the Chapel was Light

In Elba the chapel was light. Great swatches
As textured as grosgrain ribbons fell
On honey-grained pews, draped rough-stone patches,
Layered pale organ-keys with a warm pall
That softened the breath of pipes. Latches
Gleamed mute reverence; ceiling and rails
Glowed golden-arced eternity. Sachets
Breathed glory to and from embosomed walls.
Grandmother Hurd watched over us, saw all:
Whispered impatience as the hour dredged past,
Scuffled mutters of Sunday shoes on wood,
Muscles tensing for closing-prayer pell-mell
And voracious urge to break our fast—
Young souls o'erfilled, young bodies faint for food.

Operation in a Country Church

It bit, the sliver, burned to tender quick,
Slicing fingernail from moon-rise flesh.
It bit, the sliver, racing molten pricks
Up my arm, pain paired in ragged flashes.
Then deadness. Traitored nerves refused to play
Scarlet semaphores. Brain-muted echoes
Died.
    "Quick, while it's still numb," I heard him say
Softly. His bony hand gripped my elbow.
He cut, my grandfather, to tender quick,
Pared nail back to virgin, six-year flesh.
He cut, my grandfather, with his worn pocket-
Knife, deft, daring—our breath a fevered hush.

Sliver, eagle-taloned, invading me;
Strong eagle-blade to probe and let me free.

Scars

Fascinated and amazed, we watched white puffs
Of popcorn spring from husk-dried yellow kernels
Skittering in oil at the bottom of
Grandma's popper—watched with lust almost carnal,
Hot-intense, for savory soft flesh
Exploding its sparse hardness. With a quick laugh
I leaned further forward—closer—felt a flash
Of flame—*there,* gone—and saw a yellow-edged, rough
Leaf lying dead on my wrist. I plucked at it....
Even yet, the fifty-year-old pain's enough
To burst Remembery and overwhelm; but
Now the wrinkled scar beneath my stiff-white cuff
Fades under crosshatched marks from intervening
Years...scars over scars...measurements of meaning.

Summer, 1953

I was six. I wheeled grandma's milk cans
To wait, patient tin-soldiers, for the cheese
Truck. I strutted in red and black and tan
Cowboy boots. (Korea over—a grace.)

I caught six-inch whoppers—slept on rusty
Springs, waking when 40's Fords or rut-tough
Chevys crunched graveled roads—stared at gusty
Stars, my eyes not yet myopic enough
To need glasses. I rode in Grandpa's car—
Warm-stuffy grey seat-pile in front, a grip,
Translucent green, on the stiff gear-shift arm—
Four hours for a ninety mile trip.

(Sputnik was an engineer's conception—
The moon rose untouched...the Mind's creation)

The Passing of the Old Guard

Thunder mumbled over fields, echoed
Dry, warm whispers up Hollow Crick, and died.
It wasn't thunder—Dynamite burrowed
In the old stone chapel rattled granite,
Burst sound to Tower Rock, and curled back
To wade among bleak saw-toothed ruins hung
Black with a century's long breath. Pine planks
From stands three day away, floors pieced by hand...—

Now dust. Delayed roar.... The spire collapsed
Into its guts. The end. I remember
The roar, and the stone steeple as it tipped.
The new brick chapel stood fifteen years.

Today I drove by, watched steel ball and crane
Attack cracked, crumbling yellow walls, and win.

J. Roy Eames' General Store

J. Roy Eames' General Store stood red-faced
at the "Y" where asphalt curved east, gravel
ruts trickled south past Elihu Beecher's
place. Darkly solid, Eames' Store—single-gabled,
dust-warm with decades—promised quiet cool
after our two-mile hike from Grandpa's spread.
On summery days, when the sun let pool
buttered light on grey milkweed pods or hid
occasionally behind quilt-bat clouds,
Eames' Store (though adult-somber) offered still
some child-like pleasures: gum to chew in wads
stuffed in cheeks, marshmallow ice-cream cones stale
but sweet, penny candy in cut-glass jars—
and two hot miles didn't seem all that far.

Why Was the Path to the Outhouse So Long?

Twilight at Grandpa's—the sun had gone down,
We children eased in pajamas for bed;
Grandpa took hand in his rough farmer's hand—
Why was the path to the outhouse so dread?

We'd skulk down stair-steps and slip past the barn;
We'd skirt by the swing, hear the dog's low bark;
We'd tiptoe through gates night-bowered with thorns—
Why was the path to the outhouse so dark?

We'd pass by the woodpile without delay;
We'd sneak under branches bowed and leafy;
We'd hurry beyond the splintered wood-sleigh—
Why was the path to the outhouse so scary?

Panting, we'd find that we had not gone wrong—
But why was the path to the outhouse so long?

Alchemy

Bare-backed Ray, tan and dirt mingling on skin
years used to summer heat; Cleta, shorts and
fifties' playsuit-top, hair wild, uncombed, sun-
streaked; me, shorts belling over skinny tanned
legs. We three clustered around the old buck-
board—splintery and splintered wreckage years
past usefulness; we bold three conducting
secret tests far from prying eyes or ears
(while Grandma watched through age-bleached kitchen shades,
Grandpa from the shed); we three transforming
oily slicks in old Zerex cans to gold,
coaxing wine from honeysuckle berries.
Prepubescent artists in chemistry—
Now transmuted by time's harsh alchemy.

Fishing with Cousin Ray

down the No-Name-Crick that roved and rambled
past Grandma Beecher's red-brick place, on through
hip-high alfalfa to stands of ample
white-webbed willows that marked the shadowed slough
where Ray was sure the big ones hid, we three
pushed back itchy branches, forced our way to
where No-Name spread, hung catch-bags on a tree,
and began the ritual, baiting true
and straight our hooks. We cast. We dragged ripples
on smooth No-Name—and snagged our lines. Ray drew
off his pants and shoes, and—jockey-clad, stippled
with light through willowy lace, skin the hue
of sun-baked earth, adult-huge—waded out…,
mysterious as the invisible trout.

Cutting the Tree

Dad cut the fir and bound it, that late October,
Limb-tight and stiff against the northern wall
Where strait Montana sunlight could not seer
Thin needles, crust bright greens to dust-brown hulls—
Then set it in a dinted, rusted pail,
With moistened sand to feed its sap, and left
It there. The first snowfall threatened, fell—
Shrouded limbs and trunk and tin—and cleft
Green with ever-shrouding white. On Christmas
Eve, he brought the tree inside and snipped
Hemp-twine. We breathed our disappointment as
The fir stood, limb-tight and stiff, narrow-topped;
But—oh! The wonder that next Christmas morn—
Exquisite breadth of branches, light adorned—

First Snowfalls

It snowed the other day. No fragile flakes,
But rather stinging, biting darts that froze
And killed and chilled with ice flat lowland lakes
Where swans once swam, now fled from icy foes.

It snowed again. And all seemed silent, cold…,
A world of grey. No living, glistening gleam
To lighten eye or ear. No hint of gold
To grace the grave of day's last dying beam.

And once again…. But winter's night-veiled death,
Enchanted now, adorned with crystal lace,
Revives, transformed by magic, vaporous breath
To carve from fear a wondrous, light-filled place.

Now winter waits, which first stormed in as foe,
Sufficient in its power…, its soothing snow.

After Spring Rains
Billings, Montana—1958
Malibu, California—1998

Back then…when roadbeds crested concrete
Banks—and flood-tides asphalt-black invaded
Clipped, pruned lawns—and wooden rowboats swept
Inundated four-way stops to rest embedded
Against tall five-foot stoops—and sluicing mud
Remained behind to tantalize young steps
As we slipped back two for every yard we made—
Back then…cascading rains meant school would stop,
Grass gleam unmowed, weeds tower proud, unpulled—
And nowhere in REMEMBERY reside
Black-bitter images of faces paled
At damp-drowned cellars, foundation walls awade

With weeping cracks—at threatened dissolution
As sudden as a cliff-slide's deathward motion.

Father's Day:
For my Father,
and his summers spent
on active Forest-Fire Duty
with the Bureau of Land Management

Dirt-caked
ash-scoured
wood-smoke, sweat
at midnight hour.

Clothes at dawn,
heaped on the floor—
insect hulls cast on
at summer's door.

Murmurs, scents
of breakfast almost
burned, a sense
of adult loss…

then silence
and darkness.

Sputnik

Evening. Montana evening. Cool and black,
like fogged memories of a grave. Silent.
Stillness, although lights burned blue-grey in dark
living rooms, our one TV channel bleat-
ing Reddy Kilowatt's animated
weather-guess. With four kids, our home (My folks'
first home—all their own to plan, plant, and paint)—

our home must have echoed with childish jokes;

But I remember the chill and the black-
ness, looking up at stars no more my own.
"*They* have caught up," the neighbor said, breath blocked
with fear, "*They* have surpassed"—his voice a moan.
I remember chill, and the stars burned black
In the long Montana night, with Sputnik.

Hailstones

Hailstones baseball-huge pelted Billings
that July, peppered shake-shingled walls, broke
windows, shredded roofs, flayed wheat fields, killing—
pulverizing—the harvest. "Worst storm," folks
said, "in a hundred years." We didn't care.
We cowered while they welted our home, then
raced outside, collected hailstones in bare
hands chapped by summer ice. We filled a bin
in the freezer, planning to celebrate
September (but they shrank to marble-size),
piled deep rounded drifts by backyard gates,
watched balanced pyramids on porch rails rise,
stored hundreds in a cardboard box…and felt
betrayed when we discovered they would melt.

African Violets

Mabel Grafel, oldmaid schoolmarm, terror
of fifthgrade rowdies, preened rows of violets
in frigid formations on brown-veneered
tables tucked by the warmer, brighter, west-
most wall at Burlington School. That winter,
snow began in January, fell all
month. Snowplows scraped roads clean once a day. Her
pupils scuttled between iced prisonwalls

on our long treks to school. Hot-oil headbolt
heaters froze in engines; sewer lines burst;
we ran PhysEd on ice-slick sidewalks, tucked
in fur-lined parkas, freezing with each breath.
But in *her* room, rigid tabletop rings
of violets prismed winter into spring.

Second Row Behind the Deacons, Side Aisle
Billings, Montana, 1955

A lone sub-deacon on the pew—*Amens*
Pronounced—bread and water blessed to all
and then our bishop thanks/releases them
to sit with families. Two crowd—tall
lanky priests white-shirted—next to me—
in the only empty places in the hall.
I freeze. I hear thick thrumming heartbeats
of my faith—see thick man-knuckles fall
through white-starched cuffs—sneak covert glance at age—
cheeks roughened, bristling—I force a frightened caul
and drop my eyes to hands tight-clenched on gray
linen suiting—tiny hands—this nervous ball
of eight-year-flesh overwhelmed by Them …,
by flickering sight of me in ten years' time

Death on a Dirt-road Highway

"Just a flat," they said, "it was just a flat."
It killed that unnamed man on the Rimrocks
One July noon when heat-waves seemed to float
In ripples over deep-scored tire-scarred ruts;

I can imagine him driving westward,
Rattling in a decade-old forties' coupe,
Bald tires *hummm*ing, spitting gravel toward
Home, then *thumpthumpthump* as something sharp cut.

The coupe stuttered still. He removed the tire,
Felt for sharpnesses protruding inside,
Sliced his thumb as poison-flooding fangs tore
Flesh as easily as rubber. He died.

Today, a twisted branch in predawn light
Seemed a fangless rattler. My breath stole flight.

Bluebottle Flies:
Sentinel in Grandma's Attic

With grey and heavy *hmmmmm*s, a fly again
attacks the window's dust-baked pane; its wings,
two gyrous blades, distress stale air to feign
a rush of breath. *Tik-thump!* Glossy weight
bows rippled glass, and ancient apple trees
abrading splintered sills curve shadows, cut
thin fracture lines distorting buds and leaves
to knit-purl death. I slip the ancient lock
to jamb, tiptoe backward down dust-graven
stairs. That grey-toned *hmmmm* becomes a sudden
pain-pent breath. I wait. Unslip the lock. Shiver
past the door. The fly—a scrawl of dust in
Dust. Along the ledge, bluebottles crust—
Black filings flung to time's magnetic lust.

Mosquitoes

Nearly fifty years later I still smell
the heat, the dirt, the sweat—cramped and acrid
in REMEMBERY as it was in swales
carved from iron-red sandstone, where tire-skids
grooved new ruts and threw up scorching, rusty
clouds to trail us miles behind. But along
black riverflats, acres of thick raspy
reeds hid breeding-grounds. August heat re-sang

their hungry song as mosquitoes rose in
solid squadrons and attacked my father's
back, arms, hands, neck, face while he trudged to find
lost section markers. From the car, farther
from moist bogs, he seemed to fade, disappear
into a dusky, thickened, blackened air.

Mason Jars

Leafless September canes soaked in Mason
jars rinsed squeaky clean with the garden hose;
stripped and readied from last summer season's
growth, canes poised to perpetuate each rose;

By December each slept buried in snow,
one end sunk deep in cold, black soil, the other
snug beneath an invert Mason jar, so
tender cuts could withstand winter weather;

In April, we removed mud-streaked jars, saw
bronze-red leafbuds shooting on each cane, and
dug fingers in earth warm and newly thawed
to touch white, feathered roots with hungry hands—

Empty Mason jars in a basement room
earned credit for July's abundant blooms.

Sleeping in the Basement

Sleeping in the basement, alone, did not
quite live up to expectations back then,
the year I turned from nine to ten and thought
it only proper that I have my own
room, even if it was an unframed, stark-
ly concrete cubicle, bare-floored, bare-walled,
lit by a single 40-watt bulb dark

until I crossed the frigid room and pulled
its knotted cord to lighten shadows crouched
beneath the iron bedstead, the squalling
springs that shrieked harsh and ghostly if I rutched
in midnight sleep or tugged frayed quilts falling
floorward, sacrificing me to black ice.
By dawn, my shared room upstairs seemed...well..., *nice*.

Aurora Borealis

2AM and we were gently startled
from soft sleep by father's hand and mother's
voice emerging from dream-peace to herald
a wondrous intrusion of the other
into dark, dim winter landscapes. The hall
lay black before us as we stumbled to
the living room, then to the porch where all
six of us stood, unaware of cold shoes,
cold hands sticking out of thick robe arms, cold
ears and noses beneath brightly cloudless
skies. Our breath should have frozen but we held
air curdled in dry throats, watched color toss
illimitless in frozen waves to stream
arching blackness…and wondered if we dreamed.

Relay Race

Genetics decrees that eleven-year-
old boys be valleys to their peer-girls' moun-
tains. And so it was with me. Short, glower-
ing inches beneath braid-crowned heads, shy runt
among other Too-Short-Boys like my-
self, and fence-rail-thin to boot. My shadow
less than match-stick width cast on snow drifts white
as fear. No chance for equality, bond-
ing, or even simple truce with such a-

liens. So when we ran our winter re-
lays, zippered deep in fur-framed parkas, they
didn't see *me*, didn't seem to care, shriek-
ing glee as one lumbered on, knocked me down
and Jill-for-Jack concussed me, broke my crown.

Earthquake

in Yellowstone, six hours distant, late at
night, but we felt it in Billings. It rolled
us like tumblebugs on sleep-mussed beds, shot
the Fear of Good into young blood. It pulled
us and our neighbors (iron to a lode-
stone) onto dew-drenched lawns that iced our feet.
We huddled to each other, muted moods
along blank streets. One voice or two would split
the aweful silence, call a name, assure
that all was well…. Then headlights cut the night—
a week out in the boondocks, Dad drove near
enough our home to see the folks lined right
and left—to wonder at the sight of them,
that they would waken just to welcome him.

Vacant Lots

In wild green fields behind our tract we searched
long summer days for pony-herds, buried
treasures, hidden daydreams of childhood parched
by empty hours. One time I married
two neighbors in a bamboo bower, preached
vows I did not then know were parodies.
Another time we pitched ragged quilt tents
and pioneered landscaped aridities.

We sought adulthood but found instead crisp
leaves of wild lettuce shaded by tall

weeds, rambling vines with secret hoards of sweet,
long, ladyfinger grapes we chose to risk.
We built weed huts that rose in hours and fell
when parents called our return at sunset.

From the Porch [II]

From the porch, she watches silently
as I wobble down our block—ten houses
per side, each house replete with its ante
of DNA reserved for future decades
to proliferate—she watches, I wobble
side to side, slowly, far too slowly for
a twelve-year-old returning from his first
(and though she doesn't know it yet, his *last*)
stint as catcher for the Little League. She
watches, arms folded, face turned slightly,
as she has watched (will watch) in photographs—
detached, unfocused, there but not a part;
she watches but does not see red blood
crusted on my face, harsh pain-filled eyes

Twister

The tornado—*twister*—tore behind us,
not half a mile from our home. We felt
it coming first...felt its heavy, vaporous
breath spilling over grey Rimrocks to pelt
the valley...felt as much as saw its black
presaging in the west, its solid wedge
of darkness in mid-afternoon that crept
closer through absolute calm, tension-edged…
felt as much as heard its sibilant roar
as the cone first formed, then touched down behind
our tract, along the worn dirt road where clear-
cut fields lay plowed…. It roared into our minds

as we huddled in the proper basement
corner, quilt-swathed, beneath blank-eyed casements.

Drive-In

He wanted to see a Drive-In Movie,
he said, this dark-faced man whose voice even
yet speaks softly, Filipino-gently
after nearly forty years. Mom's oven-
baked chicken washed down with root-beer (hot dogs
for us kids; it was cheaper that way)—all
the trappings of an authentic picnic,
American-style, we offered him. "We'll
see," Dad temporized, scouting thick cloudbanks
over steep Montana hills. Then the sky
fell, deluge-strong. Our guest sat on his bench,
newspaper coned to keep his picnic dry.
He stuck—when wipers couldn't clear the rain—
his head out the window at the Drive-In.

Mirror Lake

"Just over the next rise," Dad repeated
for the umpteenth time as the sky drew grey
and lowered nearer raw, pine-fringed ridges
scoured to bare granite, now barred as day
receded as solemnly as promised
Mirror Lake receded with each dry mile.
It should have been only an hour or less
from camp, according to the map. Now pale
stars stared at us as we trudged our narrow
road, aiming for the next rise where we should
see reflections in its night-green hollow.
But we turned back, retraced our walk through woods
as Mother shivered. Shadowed twilight fell.
Maybe there was no Mirror Lake at all.

Peach Jam

That day the peaches ripened all at once,
Sheening gold in woven bushel baskets;
"An ox-in-the-mire Sabbath," Dad announced
As we pitched in with juvenile racket,
Stuffing quarter slices into wide-mouth
Mason jars because whole halves seemed too vast
To fit; pouring syrup—boiling, frothy
Gold; giving rings a sturdy final twist;
Then mashing bruised peach tags and broken bits
Into the well-worn grinder Mom brought out
Each summer just for jellying; licking
Fingers, peach-gold and unspeakably sweet....

We missed on church that day...a rarity;
And yet the day seems draped in purity.

Orion

Stars—once diamond-dust trails from ex-
ploding crystal balls—flicker dimly now;
Then, bright Orion marched tread-ponderous
beneath an Idaho sky. I woke—down
sleeping bag saturated by dew, bare
feet chilled, crickets echoing from green wheat-
fields—I thought I knew a true future....
And bright Orion marched ponderously.
Last night, through light-glaring LA skies, I
traced hypothetical lines, Betelgeuse
to Rigel—and saw through joints and binding
sinews to distances immortal, vast....

Suns burn in silent vacuum...diamond-rust
Tarnishes...and Orion, merely stars.

1,000,000

Counting to a million, stomach-sprawled, he
scritched number after number on his roll
Of butcher paper spread across our floor.
Night by night, the paper's essence increased
by hundreds...thousands. Smiling patiently,
Indulgently, she glances down at him, arms
knotted at her breast. His eraser mars
a misplaced number—scowling at the beast
he scritches on and on. Kitchen-bound, we
three scrub ragged rings from plates, wash pans, drop
milk-glazed glasses into hot water, prod
wrinkled fingers across smooth flatware, grease-
encrusted. We work. He scritches numbers.
We work, clean up, endure silent hours to slumber.

Sparkle

Sparkle-sparkle—gutter-light flashes once, twice.
I crouch above a thick inch-layer of dirt
raw from spring thaws, focus two excited eyes
on glistening stones, calculating their worth—
sparkle-sparkle-sparkle—not in coin or cash
but in sheer loveliness as slick root-beer glints
wink at me, beg a home. I pick them up, crush
them in my palm, quite overcome by their glanc-
ing sparkle-sparkle-sparkle—and rush to soothe
angular facets with soft cloths and polish.

The parents see, watch, take the bracelet with smooth,
practiced grasp—"Don't waste precious time so foolish-
ly"—and let me know, down through the depths of soul,
this is not a bauble *boys* should wish to own.

Sleeping Out

Beneath box-elders that by day rose striped
And mottled under thick umbrella-crowns...,
That wove stark summer's heat through leaf and twig
And dropped cool shadow to the waiting ground;
By night...by night rhapsodic melodies
Of all imagined trysting-songs breathed warmth
And whispered from the trees like memories
Not wholly understood that triggered mirth
And subtle fear as I, cocoon-tight wrapped
Against pre-dawn dew, prayed for solemn sleep
To wrest me into dreams of iced, sweet grapes
That burst their bitter skins against my thirst....
Vagrant winds caught ripe dandelion heads,
Dispersed in random darkness lonely seeds.

Edmund Homer's Bucksaw

Edmund Homer's bucksaw, needle-sharp edged,
curved like an old man's arthritic, bow-bent
back arced in pain, hung from two wooden pegs
in his grand-son-in-law's (my Grandpa's) shed;
teeth as sharp as blizzard hunger in sod-
roofed huts, pointed as drought that dried hard-red
winter wheat—hardwood bow arcs as smooth as
rainbows, rough as box-elders in the yard;

But the old box-elders fell to winter
storms...wide wheat fields lay neglected, fallow...
the old house siding-enclosed and painted
white...and Edmund Homer's antique-yellowed,
mottled blade, its twisted guys rough rust-red,
hangs useless in dead Grandpa's leaning shed

Snowdrops

Highland snowdrops burst and, blood-red, bled fresh
spring beneath black firs, lush hemlocks and pines
canting perilously along the gash
of breath-thin soil on granite valley sides;
They thrust their height. They cowered in deep shade,
elusive, haunting—granting phantom flicks
of vision. They hid behind thick snow-shapes
that grew less with each tick
of year's impatient, waiting heart. Blight red
they perched on dying matter. They seeped
vividness with bodies long since dead,
fading into shadows blue and crisply neat
so smoothly that, unknowing, hikers' boots
could crush dead stems, destroy white-figment roots.

Because Your Sister

"Because your sister shows no love for notes,
the organ will be yours when you grow up.
By right it goes—always has—to the old-
est daughter; but in your case you may step
into her place because you love music,"
she said, and did she know the forty-year-
long breach she would create and did she reck-
on in the damage done to him when she
equated *him* with *her*, son's love with
daughter's heritage, let him know without
words how valueless his soul, how beneath
contempt she held his heart and did she doubt
an instant that she spoke but simple truth,
gave him a gift...destroyed him at the root.

To Eat a Peach

O'Halloran—fat, red-neck wrinkled like
a gross of Montana winter scarves—reeks
his laughter, stands, and punches at his class
with an unlit cigar. Three o'clock recess.
Joey Kattenhorn (hawk-thin at thirteen)
disappears into the john, blocks the door
with one shoulder, changes jeans for red gym trunks—
first to imitate brash high-school football hunks
who jeer through the diamond-paned cyclone fence.
He dares to change and play baseball in shorts,
sharp ridges of his stomach bared and tan.
I escape O'Halloran—escape and run....
Maybe I can sneak into the john before
Joey, watch him strip, wish that I could dare.

Magdalene

> "Two walking baths. Two weeping motions;
> Portable and compendious Oceans...."
> —Richard Crashaw

Home breathed silence. Kitchen walls strained to hold
stale breath. I burst in. I could barely keep
my heart controlled. I heard my mother weep
a stifled, roiling groan that shattered cold
across my spine. Her grating weeping tolled
Death—father, perhaps, or husband—some pain deep
as darkness, cutting dark. But how could she weep—
weep for Dag Hammarskjöld? *Dag Hammarskjöld,*
for pity sake! This woman who neither spoke
of politics nor Congan tyranny,
nor drew a piteous, quavering breath
for any's loss, nor trembled in a cloak
of tears before or after that long day—

not even as she stood before my father's death.[2]

Slides

Granite punctures waterfalls just faintly
blue. An eternal fawn spattered heather-
dark still contemplates flight. Indian paint-
brush blooms grey-red beside dust-caked leather
boots. His hat thrown down beside a sego
lily. His light meter measuring pale
sand verbena long since transformed to seed.
His ruler inching past a rabbit's trail.

Or us—the four of us still stair-stepped—posed
on an iron fence by some forgotten
monument. Stiffly starched in Easter clothes.
lined in front of the first new home he bought....
We are captured there, with the silent fawn...
his eye and mind, dead presence not yet gone.

First Job

Molestation rings harshly in REMEMBERY—
frightens even now, rusty and obscured;
back then, the word did not yet ring with pain.
and no, it was not quite...but something close.

I remember new white jeans, tight, stiffer
than seemed comfortable—my sleek red bike
pumping toward a row of shops—storeroom shelves
where I stood stacking boxes of new shoes.

He showed it. I did not know what it was.

---

2. Dag Hammarskjöld: Swedish diplomat and Secretary-General of the United Nations, was killed in a 1961 airplane crash on a peace-keeping mission to the Congo.

He called it a *dance-belt*, explained its use.
"Try it on." I glanced toward a screened-in
alcove behind the silent racks of shoes.

I might have taken it if some hand unseen,
had not rung the hidden entry-bell.

* * * * *

When he returned, I was hard at work
stacking boxes—empty, full, I did not care,
the job was mine. Later, he came back.
He did not try again. Instead, he talked
of nervousness, tense muscles…relaxation.
He rolled the small machine across my shoulders,
down my sides, along child-thin ribs, murmured
as he worked. He touched, and smiled a secret smile.
The hidden bell rang again. He left. I
stacked boxes, numb and shaking, until he closed.
"It won't work out," he said, stripping a handful
of dollars from his wallet. "It just won't work."

White pants. Bicycle awkward against thin thighs.
I struggled home. I never spoke the ugly word.

It…A Suspicion and an Apprehension

I do not know its cause, its time or place,
Beyond a faint apprehension in old
Photographs and slides. I see in her face—
Half-turned away from us—something lost, cold,
Severed from her own throbbing flesh…. It grows
From photograph to photograph, hardens,
Congeals lines of criticism, flows
Unspoken through tight lips. Iris gardens
Reflect its presence…absence…distance…. She

Stares outward and beyond, locked in herself,
Locked out beyond herself, enclosed, no key
Remaining that can call her back…. The shelf
On which she stores her core lies dead and dark;
It has consumed her—harsh and cold and stark.

Because the Father

Because the father was not home the task
fell to her that hot July afternoon
with triple-digit temperatures to blast
heat-ebbs and -flows   She stepped outside to find
him grubbing in rank weed-beds by the fence
hands flickering in and out among stems
segregating weed from soil with danc-
ing fingertips   He stood   She stared at him

allowed her eyes to drop   His followed hers
She did not see hot flame-beneath-tan spot
his shoulders neck and cheek but mother-sure
spoke on   *You have no business wearing shorts-*
that-short-that-thin-transparent when you sweat
The heat within surpassed the sun's own heat
                                        sure
                                        burn

Nobbled as an Eagle's Claw

So Butch and I bunked our gear into
The Bomb—Dad's faded turquoise '53—
Stowed packs and bedrolls beneath the ragtop
And drove to the Sacramento River.
Tire-treads nobbled as eagle-claws crunched
River rock—we stopped—hauled gear to the beach—
Cleared a likely spot to settle in—pitched
Our tent—arced a fire pit into reach.

That day—the next—we talked, ate fire-roasted
Hotdogs—hiked bare-chested through chest-high weeds
Clogged with webs—swam naked in icy waist-
High ripples—talked through twilight's gravid fade—

The car…now rusted shadow—the shore…
Tamed and condoed—and Butch, no more…no more.

Voice from the Dust

We hadn't met for several years, although
he remained my closest friend. He came
from Denver, we from L.A. Our quick "hello"
renewed lost warmth—our friendship felt the same.

"What did you think, back then?" I must have hoped
for a neutral reply, because his words cut.
From anyone but him, I could have coped,
But his quick answer struck me in the gut:

"She scared us all. None of us ever wanted
to visit your house, much less spend the night."
I tried to speak; he carried on, undaunted,
and calmly spoke of chilling blight on blight.

And I accepted at last the doctors' claim;
my past—once thought secure—bore bitter blame.

Just Like Beethoven

Just like Beethoven, they said (at least all
but one were right to that degree—the one
referred to Mozart, but I shall give full
credit for coming close)—as if to shame
mute agonies for deafness—as if mere
comparison of me to Beethoven

would suffice to…somehow…help recover
equilibrium and pride in playing
an instrument that I will never hear
completely—dead upper ranks of flutes,
diapasons, trumpets—as if to share
my skill with his and find the vaster truth
that while we may divide deafness and loss,
his talent was of gold—but mine, slick gloss.

What Might Follow Fire

As in mirrors—empty sometimes, sometimes
Starkly dark—I see myself reflect both light
And blight, see constant plummetings and climbs,
Moments of repose transformed to frantic flight;

From window casements thick with snow I share
Children's winter play; watch springtime buds
Wax large and plump; breathe summer's pungent air;
Flutter with delight at autumn's leaf-fall floods;

Then translate—between heartthrobs—light-feathered wings
To harbingers of death, black cancer-beats,
Shadow-box fears, bone-twisting, unnamed things;
Drink fathomless despair, embrace deceits;

And know such wild extremes shape parts of me—
Discords that I may neither fight nor flee.

After Diagnosis

and I remember her at eighty-five,
wiry, white-haired (…no surprise, since she
had turned from starling-black to startled white
before she had seen twenty-four…)—that day,

though, all thoughts of dark-haired, smooth-eyed youth
had long since died into the oblivion
of white-, and vague-, and gentle-slide to death
(...still nine bland years away...)—but that day—*then*—
she huddled close to her yellowed page, one hand,
age-spotted, vaguely trembling over one
smudged lens, obscuring froth-white eye. She strained
to cipher hieroglyphic scrawls. She moaned
one time, bewailing cataracts and years.
At fifty, I now understand her fears.

Last Night I Dreamed of Empty Shelves

Last night I dreamed of empty shelves—yellowed
enamel thick as clotted, creamy scum
On pails of warm roiled milk long years ago;
Sun-curled lining papers crisped by time
flaked beneath scarred, roughened fingertips.
I knew, even as I dreamed, that once
Those shelves had swaddled china cups, chipped
Comic-plastic salt-and-pepper sets, hand-
painted Niagaras frozen on por-
celain. I woke—knew her well (at eighty-
eight). Yet in gray shadows locked before
my eyes, wide shelves stretched silent, empty
as an untouched gravel drive, a strangled
telephone that has forgotten how to ring.

My Eyes Stayed Closed:
An Essay on the Fine Art
of Poetry Sublimating Life

I woke this morning several times—each time
a surfacing from tether-dreams to taut
realities. My eyes stayed closed—my soul
engrossed in silence, vividness, and light.

The first time, I heard silence—no jitterings,
no ringing/singing/clattering—just silent dreams
beyond the reach of random sound. *My eyes
stayed closed*—I chose the dream again.

The second time I saw colors—clear forms,
Smooth shapes, sights and sounds combined
to cradle me in reassurances.
My eyes stayed closed—embracing dreams.

I face the world half-deafened, -blinded, -aged—
and wish myself again into Remembery

In Therapy Today

In therapy today I learned to say
*ashamed*embarrassed*envious** and see…
ghosts haunting web-hung rafters trapped for
memories like lies flesh-wrapped and plump
pumping life-blood to fang-flames *ashamed*—
ghosts lining dim-stretched halls palled with pale shades
of fear, sheer and biting, waiting on the joke the poke
the laugh the harassment *embarrassed*—
ghosts unborn infiltrating joys—toys taut-
wound and tense pretense unveiled and bitter
loss tossed unnoticed to dead dust *envious*—
In therapy today I learned to see.

In therapy today I learned to say….

**Some Portraits of the Poet
in Random Settled Raw-Canvas Words**

Scarred, age-blunted strangers' hands creep…silent….
Father's, grandfathers'—short, blocky farmers'
Hands that wielded pump, plow, axe, and scythe—scraped

Broad knuckles, arthritis-warped…. Planes of face
Become my sons'; glints of eyes, deep-dyed
Umber, gleam when my daughters smile.… Nose, ear,
Subtle flick of lip—these surface in my
children's children to startle breath and heart.

Double-, triple-, quad-exposures…quints-—
Aging, curling photographs, some faded
Back to gray; others fragment glints
Digital/Potential, as yet unformed—
Pixels radiating from my mystery….
My life transformed into a Stranger's History.

On First Acquaintance
with an Insulin Syringe, aet. 56

and the needle quivers — quarterinch,
eighth, sixteenth…breadth of a single thick
hair on fishbelly paleskin, skin pinched
vulnerable to the needleprick.

One muscletwitch to slide it tissuethin
between cell and cell, release milky
hormones from the islets of langerhans,
energize hot flesh's bloody sulk….

but it stops…one faint touch — it mimics
not slimneedle but knifeblade severing
stolidflesh — breath ceases — nerves panic —
sinews resist frantic levering ….

When it is over, I breathe again.
No insulin this time…no biting pain.

Gardening Taken as an Act
Of Compassionate Service

Seventy-five—but more by several
Decades now of lassitude, of wasted
Energy dispersed in weaving webs well
Girded against strains by iron-fisted

Time—seventy-five, she holds tenacious
Grasp on her small plot, her one-fifth acre,
Overlooking in-laws, grandchildren gracious
Enough to work, root out weeds from ochre

Soil—seventy-five, she haunts strong hands
That tidy edges, hawks at prey on knees
Crusted with mud, her words descend, turn, wind
Silk-strong filaments intended to freeze

Forever matriarchal bonds intact—
Each blade of grass meticulous and correct.

When the Pipes Blew

It was frigid. Horizontal gusts
Coiled and swirled, pelting roof and eaves
With stinging, winging snow. Living dusts
Hid furrows still dark with fall's dead leaves.
    Inside, windows streaked with patterned frost
Wept silently. Sills thickened as ice
Crusted deeper and deeper. Glass glossed
With cold as winter tightened its vice.
    We threw another log on the fire.
Flames crackled, warmly bright. We huddled
Beneath comforters. Flames rose higher
As logs caught. Together we cuddled,
Listened to the ice storm's bleak tattoo.

And that was the moment when the pipes blew.

Remembering the Flight of Wingless Birds

Dusk fell early that July. Pinatubo's
dust bled scarlet, ochre, gold, and saffron
through the stratosphere. Light spread oddly through
cold plate-glass planes, hung in sheaves like wheat on
oaks and sycamores, their branches stark and sere
Silhouettes snip-scissored by occluding
mass and arabesques of leaf and twig. Air
palpable, absolved of cheer, fell in sheets
on white concrete stained hell-bleached bronze; wan west
washed pale, then deepened with crisp flames of cloak-
ash fear. Silence settled slowly through soft
light. A world away, Pinatubo smoked.
He sits beyond smooth panes to count past years,
remembering the flight of wingless birds.

Darkness in the Light

It's hard to find the darkness in the light—
To squint against the sun and watch fine mottles
Spread fluid cancers across the face
Of history. It hurts. Eyes bleed blinding tears
And skin burns, squinting that way, without
An ash-dark screen to stand between the light
And you. It's hard to see that darkness
But it is there—they lie there, static splotches
Marring the bright face, disrupting
Transmissions, tugging at waves as if to
Blend dark dregs with headier infusions—herbs
And spices plucked to vivify and to delight.
It's hard to see the darkness in the light,
But it lurks there, beyond the pain, behind the weave.

After First Blooding:
In the Fragile Mind
Where Vampires Bloom

In vacances of years bleak shadows spawn;
In blackened voids beneath raw, ancient eaves
Dust rustles dead mind-spectres in dead tarns—
She moves—thin, ghastly self—and moving breathes
Isolation's voiceless lust. My lantern
Slices with unsubtle gleam, pinions shades,
Slays and—enlightening—passes. Then
Rafters heavy-hung with harmless webs
Echo crooked-fingered light...no mystery.
For that brief flash, no blood; mute peace and rest.
But edges crisp to possibility...,
And lamplight fades, and vision's sharpness gasps
Again—*o gods*—she hovers at my throat,
In vacances of years, where shadows gloat.

Lying Hand-Crossed in Her Satin Box

Lying hand-crossed in her satin box
She falls mock-peacefully asleep at last.
Her hair, pincurled and stiffly white (bleached phlox—
Crystal crushed in her winter-storm's least blast),
Glows albino in our silent, muted glare.
Her cheeks lie sunken, dark-dry-wrinkled clefts,
Dead earth twisted at an earthquake's core—
Her fingers, useless dust for Time to sift.

She lays in wait for Eternity. And we
Dry tears, sigh fears, retrain long-pented joy
To solemn reminiscences until
Guilt-haggard, we bury her in the lee
Of a box-elder bole and—suddenly, shyly coy—
Separate, to follow out her will.

Sitting on a Rock to Watch the Dawn

Sitting on a rock to watch the dawn
Reveal Riverside, after staying up
All night (a dim-faced clock squints "five"), I yawn,
I stretch, and stand—to see the invert cup
That years ago glowed blue fill with shades
Of brown and ochre. Stars don't disappear—
They haven't shown for too, too long. Light abrades
A vague horizon, chafes two eyes that blear
At struggling dots—mercury streetlights thread-
ing smoky haze. They choke and die—
Suffocating sparks of cooling lead
Dripped from a soldering iron's single eye,
Dropping into dust and smoke to die,
Dropping into dust to smoke…and die….

* * * * *

Sitting on a rock to watch the dawn
Discover Riverside, I stand straight up
When the gold-faced clock chimes five, a muffled yawn
From City Hall breathed into mists that cup
Cool pre-dawn blue. A silent hill shades
The city's heart…shadows disappear,
Slow, almost too slow. The shift abrades
No eyes, but golden veils of mist still blear
Vivid twinkle-dots that link a thread
Of boulevards. Rose-pinks-now-white die
To vibrant spots of dawn, daylight led
In triumph through the streets to greet each eye—
And no one notices when night-stars die.
And no one slips a sigh when NightStars die

Elegy

Three months of my sixth summer sleep below
Sage stones that clatter slopes from Chimney Rock,
Sweep into shallow fields where, summer-slow,
Wheat carpet-spears await fall's winnow-rake—

Three months of my sixth summer lie with her.
Dead, she laughs no more, nor weeps, nor sets
Aside the ripest tart-sweet berries in their
Stone crocks, or ice-chilled cream, or stream-crisp cress.

Three months of my sixth summer died when she,
Too, slept. I missed her. Tears that threatened storms
Have dried, aches smoothed. And only years have eased
The loss—as spring still thaws, or summer warms.

Three months of my sixth summer sagely rest—
An apple's brown-bossed core returns to dust.

Fence Posts…And Thus the Past Proceeds

A redwing blackbird ornaments narrow
Cattail blades, heat-blown and frowzy brown in
August sweat; cool marshes shrink to fallow
Pads—the redwing balances wing and wind.
A meadowlark stretches for its moment
To release a phantom song that kissed
Soft twilights decades past—still its descant
Conjures….It waits and faces crimson east.
And—*simplicity*—a rusty-throated
robin on its fence post. I should not hear
Its song for cries of tire-tread
On asphalt…but I do—and think I dare
To watch each cedar road-line cut its forms,
And pause for each new memory to be born.

In a Distant Other-When

I might have liked to live in Milton's day,
Those years he dwelt beneath St. Peter's shade;
When Jonson, Shakespeare, Donne, and more might stay
For hours at the Mermaid Inn, and strayed,
Perhaps, down Bread Street on their nightly way
Back home, reciting poems newly made;
When stacks of precious books, fresh-pressed, might lay
In open stalls, for eager minds to raid.

But then I think…of blooded swords, of knives
Unsheathed in wrath; of dying infants, burning
Towns, sparse bodies choked and black with plague,
Of ruined hopes and ruined, battered lives…;
And see in this a dim, romantic yearning,
For a never-was-time, ill-devised, and vague.

"Death, Be Not Proud"

Donne wrote it boldly centuries ago,
"And death shall be no more; Death, thou shalt die,"
His numbers strident, confident, deny
The plague that bloomed around him. Apropos
In image and in strength, his words bestow
Faith on those who even now still sigh
Their griefs and seek a greater force, defy
Death's ever-present, grimly steadfast show.

Although we count for less the force of rhyme
And look to prose to speak our deepest fears,
Our hearts still quicken, we draw a fearless breath
When someone reconfirms Donne's ageless chime
And speaks again blunt confidence that sears:
"The last enemy that shall be destroyed is death."

The Ecstasy of S. Teresa di Avila

Bernini captured it: ecstatic, wreathing
Exultation...exhalation...pain
Severing into heart and core...breathing
Moans unutterable, as if hot veins
Were suddenly transmuted into gold,
Molten ore more richly vibrant than
The golden spear the vision thrust with bold
Diligence thrice into her flesh...again...
And yet again. Sweet agony...fire-
Borne bliss.... Solid marble writhes and gasps,
Grasps in earthly elements a higher
Adoration than bitter breath can rasp:
Not in its surcease could she know true peace.
Nor would she wish such sovereign pain to cease.

Besieged
For the Lady Amera
in her doughty Castle under Seige

Thou hast wall'd me out with wood and stony hold,
Pour'd forth heav'n's waters for thy deep'ning moat,
Caparison'd thy walls with archers bold,
Rais'd up thy gates at cornet's martial note;

Whilst I, for anguisht love, have strewn my tents
Upon thy greensward, not willed my bowmen draw,
Nor catapults against thy ramparts sent,
Nor flames to force thy icéd soul to thaw;

But soon thy walls, thy stones must fall to me,
For I have right and law anent thy heart;
Forepromised, then foresworn, now thou wouldst flee
And sooner bear Sword's edge than Love's sweet Dart:

I send for you a Charger; no poor hack
Shall bear you hence when Passion's arms attack.

To the Wilds

I am gone to the woods for a cleansing breath,
For a silent thought and a velvet touch;
I am gone to the ferns to renew the path
That only their greens can faithfully etch;

I am gone to the pines, the spruce, the fir
For elegant lines in immaculate dusks,
For subtle perfumes in noon-fire air,
And sheltering roofs beneath dawning masks;

I am gone for the lichens, the comforting moss,
The splinters of granite that, glistening, cheer;
The crunch of dense cones as I cautiously pass,
The fragrance of humus when the breeze lays it bare;

I am gone to the woods for a cleansing breath
I am gone to the wilds to renew my path.

Anamnesis

Each time I stalk the valley's graveled road,
Pause near the creek that cuts the yard
In twisted ribbons only to explode
White fury beyond the bridge, I feel a shard
Of potent loss, as if my life had flowed
With passing currents, transformed to something hard
And brittle—long years become a pressing load,
Heavy with dead weight, dismaying, scarred.

It pains. Yet still I hearken to that place—
Green canopies of leaves where once I played,

Laughing echoes no murky age can churn—
Strong icons heartless time cannot erase.
All around, the past persists, decayed;
Each time I leave, I know I will return.

Envoi: Return to the Homestead

Beyond timeworn sage-crests (grey-green outcasts
shaded by Chimney Rock) stretch hedge-quartered
fields. South, the gash of Hollow Creek etches
aspen-burnished flanks above farms toward

Albion Road. The asphalt curve angles
narrow arteries of sage, cuts the west
edge of Grandpa's farm near where an algae-
glutted slough that was Hollow Creek widens.

Once, hard red winter wheat bearded fields,
whiskered old Albion Road curled across
the valley to the mouth of Hollow Creek;
Once one-room cabins nested in grey cups

edged with sturdy sage and mountain lilac,
and rode the rolling slopes from Chimney Rock....

*****

No new folk come to farm; they buy red brick
houses…ignore wide pastures neglected
in the scowl of Chimney Rock; they guide slick
RV trailers where horse-drawn wagons rattled

up Hollow Creek, now repossessed by sage;
sego lilies and russet paintbrush creep
alien-cold to the snaggle-torn ledge
of Chimney Rock. In the valley, shadows leap

from farm to dying farm, scatter twilight
darkness like seeds upon bone-dead orchards—
I drive beneath Chimney Rock and look right
and left at wombs of bone-white, weaving sage.

In remembery I tromp green fields...
I do not look beyond grey mountain folds.

Epyllion in Anamnesis II

Taliesin

Dedication
Taliesin to Brother Prayer

Speak, good brother, in your own rhythms,
in your internal music tuned to external cadences,
your stories of the princeling Arthur

weaning himself for battle with the dark,
keening sorrow at youthful fault;
Speak, good Taleteller, in words

the commons use. You have no need to
share my iambs, borrow from my heritage of
metaphor—your voice is clear and sound and strong.

[Stronger now, in this flat world without poetic soul,
than mine: far-reaching, telling truth
as Story that reveals its larger Truth.]

Speak, good Friar, let your crafted words
echo across the continent and declare
another Arthur, another Avalon

in crystalline dreams. Let your modulating voice
Blend strains of red and white, green and brown,
white and black...create anew my Arthur

as your own, your Arthur to become
my own, our own to share with all the worlds.
Speak, good brother, who once mastered

song and now—through choice—elevates
pure speech to incorporate the living cadences
and rhythms of the deeper Song subsuming all.

Taliesin to His Harp

"An Arthur! An Arthur! We have
An Arthur!" echoes ivory-colored halls
and untouched shelves creaking silently
beneath the pall of unread tomes

and popular images and garish cartoons
and computer-animated feature-*fabliaux* and

raucous voices explaining expanding
enhancing enlarging by diminishing....

And yet I would have another Arthur,
speak another Arthur woven in eastern
Avalon, weaving western Avalon in
another place, another time,

another timelessness that undercuts
pretentious haughtitudes—as if the Arthur

of my heart were somehow less *real*
than vain imaginings excreted by minds

that no more *believe* the core of Story than
allow that Story to caress their core
and change them and define them and in
so doing refine them and exchange

icon for ideal. I would sing an Arthur
who can feel and breathe and live and

change forever the Camelot he would build.
I would sing Williams' Arthur, and Lewis's,

and more—I would sing the myth incarnated,
the legend and the lore impassioned, passing
myth-like through the reins of history and
passing, changing, changing, changing.

I would sing an Arthur.
I would sing a new unchanging entity

Both symbol and reality, both king and King.
I am Taliesin, of Arthur's court, and I would sing.

Taliesin to Light

Did you understand, Light, the burden
you chose in bearing him?
Did you understand, Light, the cost
in heartache, sorrow, grim

sparring with death and darkness?
Did you hope, Light, for that joy
beyond all joy, the mortal vision?
Did you hope, Light, for your boy?

Did you weep, Light, blood-dark tears
when Merlin touched him with deep dreams?
Did you weep, Light, green-shadowed tears
when daylight bowed to silver moonbeams

and dreams consumed the son you bear?
Did you rise, Light, with damp dawn
and press your hand against your unborn son?
Did you rise, Light, with the Dawn?

The Solstice-Born

Nearly so, so nearly cusped against the back
Of summer, breast of winter—for perfected
Symmetry but two days lacking;

Sufficient, though, in one who bore no need
Of incarnational symbology—
And near, so near the winter Seed

That sprouted prefigurements and completion.
Solstice-born, he who adds, who would add,
Who will add through his subtraction

Present absence, absent presence.
Ice ridges and wolf cries welcomed him
Pine boughs and wood smoke offered incense,

Nearly so, so nearly cusped against the breast
Of balanced winter-year, ice-crystal kissed.

Taliesin Recounts the Wound
to Arthur's Leg

It might have been an arm, a shoulder blade,
A rib (the thirteenth, harkening to its mate),
A hip-joint traitor-turned to cowled leg,
Or even an eye obscured by unseen mote;

It could have been any of these, his body
Turned against the man-soul inhabiting,
But it was his leg, infected badly,
Microscopic darkness orbiting

Blood, destroying it—that simple—to kill
The King before his crown could fit full forged.

But excised—bone cut out with bloody skill—
Removed, the sickness could no longer gorge

Itself on him, and died. Wounded, healed, lamed,
He bore its lifetime-scars, this Fisher-King.

Arthur and the Head of Bran

In the last hour of his childtime, Uther's
Son braved Tower Hill alone to find out
For himself what enduring powers there be.
Secluded under trees sacred to gods
From times beyond living memory, he
Exhumed the head of Brennius, studied
Its worm-smoothed brow.   Wide as imagined seas,
The skull stared hollowly. Knowledge eddied
Through Uther's son: "Bran has no eyes, no ears,
No mouth. He cannot speak green truth, listen
To revolving prayers rising, see tear-
Sacrifices in valiant hearts."   He hastened
From Tower Hill, eyes afire, breast aflame,
Voiceless skull in hand...*Arthur* announced God's Name.

Taliesin to the Stones

RingStones stand silent   aslant in wasted lands
beyond the Plain.   once they spoke/sang/rang—before
the oldest memories of Oaks   beyond
bloodSongs of bloodThirst-worship staining earth

I stand and search dim/dark horizon lines—
bones long brittle rise/rage/urge my quest for
Song *beyond the Plain*   ancient Bardic bones,
Heroes' bones, witnesses of War—weary War.

My fingers ply their stringless lyre. Voice

Beseeches silence—demands ears—invokes
Gods lost/forgotten/
               / hoped-for/
                        /*feared.*
                                 Face
And hands and body weave the Shape of Hope.

Soon.
    Soon.

            But now the Stones—the Land—the Song
Await.
      I feel it breaking—trembling Dawn

Taliesin and the Kings

Other kings arose before this King—
Princes, princelings hungry for a crown,
Eager for raw-valiant thrill of waging
War against the immortality of Rome.

Other kings—chieftains, tribal heroes, strong
Men of courage, lifting weapons, raising
Voice-pitched flames against the Dark that long-
Too-long concealed our coming King-to-Be.

Other heroes—earlier—sought to draw
The sword, grasped its gilded haft with bone-bare
Hands long used to manhood and men's awe—
Raised it but the breadth of one coarse hair.

Other kings approached the Blade-in-Stone—
But none could draw it fully…no…not one.

The Grail

hidden beyond westward mists and sun-sleeps,
beyond waves of grasses green-brown ripe, and
hunched flanks of mountains, and roiled streams deep
with life, it sleeps also and dreams and sends

its dreams in dreams to Arthur where he lies
wide-eyed on a garret bed beneath rough
hand-hewn shingles that weep yet sticking tears
and glimmer lightness, dim but still enough

to catch his waking dreams and cast them high
as mountain pinnacles and reflect them
in six-spired elegance and draw from eyes
that see beyond rough shingles to the one

tears unspoken for the vessel and blood
of Christ, granite-encased for Galahad.

Arthur and Guinevere

West and south, where fabled silvered metals
    Rested (or were hoped to rest) in rich earth,
He journeyed, not just to solve their riddles
    But to bring beauty to his granite hearth—

Instead of buried silver, raven locks;
    Instead of dark-clasped secrets, hazel eyes;
Instead of harsh earth-scrabbling, heart-felt looks;
    Instead of metal hoards, love-promised ease....

She journeyed north and east with him, this bride,
    To share his visions of the City soon
To bloom. She bore him children, living and dead;
    Transformed coarse tents into a mansion-home.

But when he fell, and we pursued his dream...,
She stayed behind, and would not follow him.

Taliesin Considers Excalibur

It was no woman's arm that bore his sword
    Weeping upward from an ice-placid lake
    To arm him for blood-battles yet to come—
His weapon wore the biting edge of words.

It did not come to him, this life-shield sword,
    Sweeping upward from still, watery rest;
    He dug for it, removed it from its stone store-
Place, redeemed it with his warm, breath-locked words.

It was no glistering, steel-shaft faerie sword
    Sleeping sightless, beyond Time's history;
    His the vision, the graver mystery,
That from archaic dust formed sun-sharp words.

It was no woman's arm that wore his sword—
His weapon bore the biting edge of words.

Arthur and the Serpents

They gathered in tight knots around three snakes—
Coiled, sinuous as dragon's-breath—rude men
Prodded diamond scales with blunt-tipped oak sticks
Torn from nearby trees...once straight, living, green;
Men prodded, stirring dumb serpents to wrath,
Then poised on the edge of slaughtering them,
As if awaiting his permissive word—

Instead he held his warriors back; a dam
Across floods of fear and anger, he warned
Against thoughtless death. Later, one cold night,

One knight awoke to find a serpent warmed
Beside his cheek.
                    "And thus at peace, no fight
Between them, they shared a bed," he said; and
None could know which was Lion, which was Lamb.

Taliesin and Arthur's Majesty:
At the Founding of the City

I have witnessed his majesty in lands
   none living would possess, in wilderness
     wastes rejected and reviled—lands he blessed
with vast visions and mild words of command;

I have witnessed his majesty in swamps,
   pestilent, malarial, where each breath
     bred fever-chills, delirium, and death—
his touch evaporated deadly damps;

I have witnessed his majesty in tents
   mildew-mottled, torn, ravaged by winds
and rains—encampments baser than base sins
he fought, transformed to godly monuments;

I have felt his raw silk handkerchief laid
on hot flesh...my self retrieved from the Dead.

Taliesin's Vision of the Wondrous Pillars
Supporting Arthur's Halls

One, three, ten, scores—they rise as seedlings rise,
Fragile at first, susceptible to each
Fluctuation in warm earth, in moist skies;
Then—tentative—unfurl stark leaves and reach
To emulate mute prayer. Their natal ties
To solid rootstocks falter, fail. They breech

Into bright open space and breathe their prize,
Exalted almost into mortal speech;
    But no, these are not growths of wood and bark—
No apples brought from distant Avalon,
No fragrant peach—these pinnacles of stone
Emerge from Arthur's vision-eye; they mark
Extent and boundaries from night to dawn…,
They represent the life-blood in his bone.

Arthur Blesses a Faithful Knight

And the City was begun, stone on stone;
Timber splayed to timber with square, hand-forged
Nails; smooth pavers sealing ruts that gouged
Red furrows in the City's native bone;
And Arthur stood upon a prominence
Some way away and watched the City shape
And swell, and pondered on his hidden hopes,
In awe as Vision's contours formed to Sense.
Éadmond, standing near, saw Arthur lift
Calm eyes. He raised one coin in his own gaunt
Hand: "To share the Visions that you see."
"You MAKE the City rise with this, your gift—
Nor you, nor your children's blood shall ever want."
Thus was it spoken, thus it came to be.

Taliesin and the Questions

I chose to let the questions rest unasked
although I knew…believed…hoped he had sensed
true answers. Instead I joined him at tasks
I had disdained. In conscious ignorance
we waited by white City gates to greet
arrivals at their journey's end; we bound
gangrenous wounds, excised embedded shot
with penknife tips; we raised dippers moon-round

and glistening to lips that thirsted for
more than water; offered smiles to hearts thrust
down by mobs, to eyes inured to salt-tears,
tongues longing to taste simple words of trust—
    For months we wept our self-appointed task;
    I chose to let the questions rest unasked....

Taliesin Witnesses the Commission to the Table

Twelve rose from his table, knelt to receive
    His blessings, faded into waiting night
    Leaving him alone to raise white walls, save
The City from flowing onslaughts of hate;

Twelve stole their way to the grey cornerstone
    Lying dust-shrouded, belying blood-spoor toil
    To roll it from earth-shadows without stain;
Twelve prayed, departed, questing for their Grails—

They would win strong workers for the City
    In distant kingdoms. Twelve families lay ill,
Some dying, all hoping. From the jetty
Arthur stared unblinking Eastward. A pall

Darkened low hills...but he saw only Dawn—
New Sunrise—and twelve Table-Knights' return.

Arthur and the Mountains

On two *Badon*s he conquered, the first climbed
Stone by stone, four times—ascending over
Echo-bones of war-men long ages dead,
Reaching through bleached remnants for victory.

The second he saw in dream-time visions

But conquered yet, gazing westward, white face
Glowing in red mountain-sunsets only
He could see. From the plains—*"Beautiful Place"*
On the river—he alone could taste
Hot sweat, smell pure blood his people must shed
Before they reach wild desert Grail-Wastes,
Penetrate granite battlements.
                                    Broad
As memory, his Valley lapped Badon's
Roots, peaceful beneath harvest-gold shadows.

Taliesin Reacts to Arthur's Revelation

He has counseled me to wed another
    art, this King who long consumed my words with
    eager hunger, nourished his sovereign heart
on rhythms intricate as misted breath
    that permeates thought-convolutions of
        blood, mind, soul. He has counseled me to wed
    another art, to share my single love
with another bride—betray beloved words.

How can I not act according to his
    will? how turn my back on his voiced command?
        But what he asks is harder than cold stones,
    or bearded ice that cracks on river strands—
As easily could I love two women
equally, as sever from my sole song.

Arthur's Great Hall

It was to be perfect...the perfect place:
Sun-stones, Star-stones, Moon-stones, Spire-columns to
Pinion Earth to Sky, pull Time down, embrace
Vast space between Here and Eternity;

It was to be his citadel: marbled
Mountain cresting his City's future folds;
It was to house his chosen Knights' Table,
Without Beginning and without an End;

It was...and was not. Even before walls
Rose sunset-high, before roof sparkled with
Dew, before squared pillars bore weight of ills,
His City lay beleaguered by black wrath,
His perfect place lay flayed as Evil's home...
And he lay silent in his secret tomb.

Taliesin and the Lamb

Some whispered him a traitor, even those
whose lives cross-linked with his in blood and flesh;
Some spoke out quickly to condemn his rash
setting off alone on dark western quests;
Others jibed against his courage, called him
"Coward," "Thief," who stole their faith and hearts, set
out without them across wide rivers, pit
his Self against their greater pain...and won.

I crept behind him in morning shadows—
heard his heart break for Camelot, now doomed;
saw her slash his heart with accusations;
felt him swim against black-prophetic gloom,
stare at silver flecks in vatic waters,
sigh himself to death...our lamb to slaughter.

Taliesin Bemoans His Loss of Words

How can I sing his death, though I was there?
   Forced, final night shock-charged with his sorrow
   For all that would be lost with the morrow—
How could I sing that night, though I was there?

How can I sing his death, though I was there?
   Hushed voices sharing a solemn, subtle hymn,
   Him joining as small hours of blood-life dimmed—
How could I sing that hymn, though I was there?

How can I sing his death, though I was there?
   Rushed, frantic rout of traitors garbed in grey,
   Vile act of darkness eclipsing bright day—
How could I sing that darkness, though I was there?

How could I sing his death—*last moments flare...*
Harsh bullets rip his flesh—though I was there?

Taliesin at the Grave of Arthur

Ten thousand mourners flowed beside his bier,
Sorrow beyond words measured in dull, slow,
Still tread—in unashamed, unnoted tears—
And where his body rests, they do not know....

At evening, bluestone doors slid closed. Those few
Blood-linked removed his corpse. In fear of foes
Maddened for revenge, they hid him from view—
But where his body sleeps, they do not know....

At midnight, I guarded his secret grave.
Heaven opened. Summer rains overpoured
Their bounds, buried black portals to the Cave—
And where his body sleeps, I only know....

Taliesin Overlooks the Ruins of Camelot

And now that he is—not dead, no, but *passed,*
departed—now that his shadow no longer
stripes the streets of his glory...what is left
from this height, to see, to taste in anger?

And now that he is gone, where is the whiteness
on the hill? or stone suns and moons and stars
he willed to *be*? and they were as his breath
rising, sacred fires from honest hearths.

And now that he is gone, what is the cost
of our tears? the savor of our silence?
why prolong the agony of these ghost-
walls waiting doom and bloody violence?

Only this—that partings unsubstantial
Heighten joy in promised, hoped renewal.

Arthur's Knight Returns the Blessing

Éadmond rode into the ruins of Arthur's
Place, stared at fire-gutted walls, at ways
Bereft of smoothing stones, of heartening ease…,
He saw the *Beautiful Place*, and wept for her.
He gasped out breath of Over-Sea and drew
In poison-misted fogs, breathed fever-marsh
And torture-bog spread over the land in harsh
Ungoverned grasps. He wept the pain he rued.

But in one hall—miraculous remain—
He found the Scribe squatted in torn shade,
Averring the songs that Taliesin sang.
"Come now with me," he pled, "Across green Plains,
Share Arthur's dreams." "I have too long delayed."
"No. Come." And Arthur's towers in triumph rang.

Taliesin Contemplates the Vanity of His Works

Arthur *bled* his Grail-Hall—I merely sang a score,
Two-score…, and more…, through gyring generations
Since he slept; I sang curved, scaling towers,

Subtle intricacies of Time and Stone;
I soared spun-pinnacles beyond massed clouds,
Seared images in celestial shadows
Behind my eyes, wove majesty aloud
In each taut line, each breath, each melody.
And yet...constrained by weight...my Grail-Songs fade,
Falter, fall to utter silence and to death
Of Song. Tears well. Sounds choke. Breath stops. Sight—frail
With age—begins to fail. One with Earth,
I commence stern closure of my dreams.

Yet Arthur's Hall still stands...it is, not seems.

Taliesin Dreams of Seagulls

Yesterday I heard a distant seagull
Cry and, glancing skyward, saw dream-white
Touched with charcoal-ash arc above [...,] small,
Deft sounds of feathers ruffled air. Too late
I focused—by then it had diminished
To a fluted cry, brief echo against
Unbroken blue. [...] Too late, it flashed
Once more, so far removed it seemed to test
Sheer memory—a flash, a moment's grace
Urging plaintively beyond a linen
World. [*...and gone.....*] It carried into time, space,
Eternity a single fading glint
That I shall now encase in brittle glass,
Immure in beds of browning, bitter moss.

Taliesin Writes an Elegy for a Swallow

I watched them whirl—an indeterminate rout—
Beyond the lintel, flared feathers flashing
Silver-and-grey, seeming-black beneath clouds
Piled up offshore before invading

The Coastal Range. I watched them swirl and hurl
Themselves on invisible currents—twist,
Arc, pivot, rise, and fall in immeasure-
Able rhythms that avoided close-massed
Bodies of fellows diving for similar blobs
Of mud to build quaint nests. I watched them hook
Against rough stucco, press minute daubs
Into their growing shells, then wing back
Down—their numbers swallowed half the sky.
I did not watch this single swallow die.

Taliesin Mourns for the Pelicans

From shore, the rock hunched white and sodden, drowned
By whorls of spray, softened to mottled grays—
After-sunset-pearls. *Something moved.* Down
They dropped, black kernels knotting darkness, day's
Tears—dark-on-white—plashing against bone-rock,
Skull-rock craning up, around, enticing
Waves. They dropped, spiraled, settled on the back
Of that single white-washed promontory
Half-a-hundred yards beyond dull cliffs. One,
Then two, then four—they singly stroked the wind
To find each place of settlement—alone,
Disparate on the rock's rutched arc, they dined
On half-digested fish. *This year, four eggs,*
Bone-china-thin, lay shattered in stick nests.

Taliesin Broods on the Order of Succession in the Corruption of His Memory

Once I could have named their Order: The One,
The Three, The Twelve, The Seven (threes and fives
And sevens in precise Uptonian
Display)—named his Successors through the wave
Of shock-white hair presiding over decades.

I could have tolled their names in sequence, order,
Firm precise controlled—sung my Davids
Josephs—mourned the passing of my Reubens—
And Named with the sureness of foresight
The coming Order as I waited
Patiently through prophecies of dates
And pretenses of Symmetry and Time.
   No more. Blurring shifts of time and memory
   Have hollowed me of hope and clarity

Taliesin to His Solemn Self, in His Old Age

Almost deaf and almost blind I sit—
I would sing…and I cannot. I would strike
Loose harpstrings…and my traitor fingers knot
And clench and will not move. I feel bright aches
Of notes unsung, of blinding sunlight rare,
Casting darkness on bleared eyes. And I wait
To hear their words, the Heirs of Arthur's Heirs,
From the veiled shade of Arthur's sky-stone heights—
Lips long lost to vatic throbs murmur sounds;
Eyes long dimmed mist purer, loftier lights;
Ears long closed shunt all but piercing clamor....
And yet…and yet…heart-faint blood-echoes pound
Deft rhythms; faint stars sprinkle vasty night;
*And hope…*Hope*…wings unhampered evermore.*

I Have Set my Feet

I have set my feet upon greyed
Dust-crowned grass girding faint trails
He (only in his Visions!) trod—

I have felt warm winds roughen hills
Across breath-brittle plains, and known
His People's footsteps as they've filed

Past palisaded walls stained brown
With sweat and blood—known the heart-flint
Ache of shallow graves and shattered bones

Consigned behind—mute testaments
To words haunt-echoing thin air
As he departed on Western winds—

And I have felt his sole presence near,
Stepped in their footsteps, drunk their tears.

Taliesin to Autumn

Full-moon light on flat fog-dewed meadow-runs—
Gilt chrysanthemum, red spider-lily—
Thrush and wild geese high in the wind-blown sky—
Grasshopper's whirred flight and cicada's thrum—
Sun-crisped oak leaves greet twilight with a hum—
Milky weed-down of thistles cluster by—

These I have seen, these I have—ceaseless—sung
Until my eyes, my songs grow harsh and dry….
But in chrysanthemums lodge dreams of cherry
Blooms… Fog and dews weep springtime freshets cold…
Tides that ebb will flow again at last…
And crisp give way to falling-blossom berry—
So I await sweet plums, though I am old,
Though Arthur's Pilgrimage overtakes my haste.

And Yet the Stones Endure

Years cast themselves against dressed stones,
Brittle, coarse, angry, and afraid.
They summon winds to chafe, abrade,
Grate smooth polish to pitted bones
Of stair-steps, walls—staid monuments

To long-past energies decayed.
They summon storms to wash away,
Grain by grain, thick grey cements
Until each stone lies separate,
Black hollows isolating each,
Waiting for winter's ice to leach
Final strength, make each desolate.
   Yet still the stones endure, stairs climb,
Walls hold…defying death and time.

Envoi: Taliesin's Testament

If you have lived these verses well, remember
I was Taliesin, once Arthur's Bard;
In my mouth, EARTH and AIR trans-shifted, FIRE

with WATER intermixed. In life I heard
His voice speak Mysteries, Visions word-clothed;
In his defense I emptied out my hoard

Of Poetry and scattered—nothing loath—
All of my self upon four questing winds.
In that lay immortality, that both

Of us extend beyond our times, expand
(Me through seed-words, he through root-prophecy),
Bud green, and burgeon in the soil of minds.

His voice and mine recall his STORY's splendor;
And you who live these verses well, remember....

ELEMENTAL SONETS

Elemental Sonets

[*Any juxtapositions—real or perceived, meaningful or fanciful—between the Elemental Sonets and their accompanying texts exist only in the mind of the Poet. Nothing is implied about the fundamental beliefs of persons quoted. All implications, extrapolations, suggestions, or possibilities created by the juxtapositions are my responsibility.*]

For James, who understood…

For Scott, who inspired…

And always…for Judi…,

Who loves and endures—

The elements of all…propertics or things are eternal, uncreated, self-existing. Not one particle can be added to them by creative power. Neither can one particle be diminished or annihilated" [Parley P. Pratt]

Elementals

Elementals live, have-lived, will-live—all
Then and now and yet-to-be—without
Beginning/End—no breaks to smooth dark palls
Upon their biers, however brief; no doubt
That what is was—was, is—and always yet
Potentially. Once there seemed four (or five,
Perhaps) quintessentially—well-met,
In infinite proportions mixed, alive,
Ascending-and-descending through staid spheres…,
Now scores arranged in periodic grace
But still enduring endless course of years,
Time-tumbled elements in unceasing race.
Surfacial shifts may flow their take-and-give;
But elementals live, have-lived, will-live.

* * * * *

Earth, stars, and the vastness of space; yesterday, today and tomorrow, with the endlessly increasing knowledge of the relations of forces, present an illimitable universe of numberless phenomena. Only as a whole, and in general outline, can the human mind understand the universe. In its infinite variety of expression, it wholly transcends the human mind.

Man in the Universe. In the midst of this complexity, man finds himself. As he progresses from childhood to manhood, and as his slumbering faculties are awakened, he becomes more fully aware of the vastness of his universe and of the futility of hoping to understand it in detail.

Nevertheless, conscious man can not endure confusion. Out of the universal mystery he must draw, at least the general, controlling laws, that proclaim order in the apparent chaos; and especially is he driven, by his inborn and unalterable nature, to know if he can [establish] his own place in the system of existing things. Every normal man desires and seeks an understanding of his relation to all other things, and practically every man has worked out for himself, on the basis of his knowledge, some theory which explains, more or less satisfactorily, the mystery of star and earth and man and life. No other quest is followed by man with such vigorous persistence as that of establishing an intelligible and satisfactory philosophy of earth life. [John A. Widtsoe, 1-2]

Matter exists, perhaps, in many forms, but may be classified as the ponderable matter of earth, known directly through the senses, and as the imponderable matter which cannot be sensed directly by man. This second class, often called spirit matter, is perhaps the most important, for it is not unlikely that from it are derived all other forms of matter. [John A. Widtsoe, 29]

Creation:
On Considering the Imponderable Matter of the Universe

unmade protons sigh//transform   translated
electrons/positrons   attenuated
particles managed by magnetic fields
forage through infinity   counsel   yield
consent to constitute each Entity,
time and space slow to full eternity…,

ENTITY   galactic-huge organic
thought unable yet of peace or panic
sweeps meditative prescient-memories
to chemistry   physics   cosmology
twists subatomic particles their fraction
with each inarticulated action

moves INTELLIGENCES a millennial nod
and contemplates imagining its GODS

* * * * *

    First. THEOLOGY is the science of communication or of correspondence, between God, angels, spirits, and men, by means of visions, dreams, interpretations, conversations, inspirations, or the spirit of prophecy and revelation.
    Second. It is the science by which worlds are organized, sustained, and directed, and the elements controlled. [Parley P. Pratt, 15]

MoonMasks

MoonMasks shelter pending loon-Worlds/swoon-Worlds—
whorled inFinitely darkRinged quarkWinged pin-
paint Stars   inefFable slit/fit against
entrenched plight/flightless pit of shudder/night

floating MoonMasks wash skies fundamental
sacramental pitch skies with repeated
heated amply varied blurs of spin-white
night-flight greys   shadowed lights circling Earth

wan MoonMasks disclose   oppose gravities—
concavities collapse   lunarchic coaches
link cosmic levity to star-ghost shapes

draped lasered forms beyond sky-dark-sight-blank

MoonMasks reveal deeper blazy shocks
mock fear...and sheen dull earthy-radiant rock

* * * * *

To speak more philosophically, all the elements are spiritual, all are physical, all are material, tangible realities. Spirit is matter, and matter is full of spirit. Because all things which do exist are eternal realities, in their elemental existence.

Who then can define the precise point, in the scale of elementary existence, which divides between the physical and spiritual kingdoms? There are eyes which can discern the most refined particles of elementary existence, there are hands and fingers to whose refined touch all things are tangible.

In the capacity of mortals, however, some of the elements are tangible, or visible, and others invisible. Those which are tangible to our senses, we call physical; those which are more subtle and refined, we call spiritual.

Spirit is intelligence, or the light of truth, which filleth all things.

Its several emotions or affections, such as love, joy, etc., are but so many actions or motions of these elements, as they operate in their several spheres.

By these actions or emotions the elements manifest their eternal energies, attributes, or inherent powers.
[Parley P. Pratt 50-51]

Volcano

Heat beneath   beat beneath   convulsive heat/
beat/retreat of fire   thrum/drum/sun-hot cen-

ter   polar/pillar penetrates sensate
liquid ore/core   heat beneath below
                                            man-
tled bone-fire/stone-fire/bonfire of vagar-
ies   " '*ante Vulcunum*,' before fire, art-
ifice, and the yoke of labor"[3]   knee-arc
finger-curl shoulder-roil above new-heart-

beat RISE face flesh furnace/blasted new RISE
eye-flame throat-flame neck-flame RISE beyond fire
already pooling golding gilding mass
in open space in CONDENSATION
                                          cool-air
savors heat   assuages beat transmuted gold
weds leaden-darkness-crusted-Earth-moist mold

* * * * *

    God spake, and the worlds were framed by His word.
    He spake, darkness dispersed, and light prevailed.
[Parley P. Pratt, 17]

Air

h e a v y   torpid   air   soils lungs with lead
boils black from asphalt cracks sidewalks chalk-
encrusted— rusted handbars scorch hands red
worn-rubber swings reverse fierce fretful jerks

sole-motion   slow-motion arcs   sun-bleached park-
scape shimmers motionless against the line
horizon-distant spume of hunching black
en-trop-ic   hor-i-zon-tal   anodyne

---
3. Raphael Falco, 148

drags breath   drags bone blood sinew sweating brow
eyes-upward   -northward   colliding black on
black [...]   s i l e n c e   [...]   pent breath in a blow
funnel-tunnel twist-stalk shearing golden
after-light spume-bright-essence whirlwind-fear
grain-threshing flesh-crushing swirl-rushing air

Tornado
Montana, 1959

Brittle light—stark bright yellow—stark blighting
blackness in the West—heavy electric
air   stills   birdsong—silences July
afternoon. Something—Coming—Soon—. Scalp-itching
eye-twitching weight—Unnamable—. Something—
Soon—. When it comes   relief almost   until
wind-fingers hook gray shingles—frightened clinging-
-huddle with silent basement spiders—while

unseen-but-heard spiral winds to summer
frenzy—dreadnought whine blots all sounds. And then
studded with twisted limbs like ragged spears
it dies—drops—silver-twilit black-slicks blend—.
Rows of wood-shake Homes shudder at its death—
Raw Wheatfields draw low gasps of shattered breath—

* * * * *

...Brothers Heber C. Kimball, Geo. A. Smith and I went to London together in the winter of 1840, being the first Elders who had attempted to established the gospel in that great and mighty city.

As soon as we commenced we found the devil was manifest; the evil spirits gathered for our destruction, and at times they had great power.

> They would destroy all the Saints if they were not restrained by the power of God.
>
> Brother Smith and myself were together, and had retired to our rest, each occupying a cot, and but three feet apart.
>
> We had only just lain down, when it seemed as if a legion of devils made war upon us, to destroy us, and we were struggling for our lives in the midst of this warfare of evil spirits until we were nearly choked to death. [Wilford Woodruff, 95]

Naked on Its Branch the Shadow Stands

Naked on its branch the shadow stands
Bulks sulks sits flits flirts shifts
With every wending of a-pillow-Sun
Now-lean now-wan now-harsh now-elemental
Gental rolling hills and emerald swards
No-high behind beyond beside beneath

And the shadow remains, rests
Bulks sulks sits flirts flits shifts
With each warning of the moon-diame-
ter try thrive throw spin-dinning frenzies
Other-shadows other-silence other-milk-marsh
Banks slip salient streams course onward
Outward downward from the branch-raw
Crotch where the shadow stands

Hombres, Mexico
Photograph by Sebastiào Salgado (1980)

mud in black and white   rich ephemeral
mud emerging temple steps beneath feet
shagging black-and-grey quickmarch up death's-hill
slick-steep   black-mud-rimed hands clench roots in hate

knotted thighs calves serpentined into black mud
black blood caking calluses white-raw scars…
centered one stiff leg presses mud-clogged tread
mottle-stripped-barkless treetrunk spears mud stairs

backs arch taut sweat-sticky-grey sharp elbows
arc awkward angles   black hands grasp black mud
white-glowing light   buttocks tensed   ankles raised
torqued twisted   sodden mud-black socks flayed

but no shoulders   necks solid with black stresses
no head brain mind   no black-and-white grained faces

* * * * *

  Biblical lore and ancient tradition among nearly all of the races of man, tell of the 'fall' of the first parents from the grace of God. An event called the fall did occur, but it was a necessary part of the Great Plan. Adam and Eve were eternal beings, and were not under the ban of mortal death. Subject to death they must become, however, if their posterity should inherit corruptible bodies. The fall was simply a deliberate use of a law, by which Adam and Eve became mortal, and could beget mortal children. The exact nature of this event or the exact manner in which the law was used is not understood. The Bible account is, undoubtedly, only figurative. There was no essential sin in the fall, except that the violation of any law, whether deliberate or otherwise, is always followed by an effect. The 'fall' of Adam and Eve was necessary, for without it there would have been no begetting on the earth of spirits with mortal bodies, and the Plan proposed and confirmed in the Great Council would have remained inoperative. 'Adam fell that man might be.' [John A. Widtsoe 47]

Falling Water

Falling water cuts cold granite at its
Precipice—severe   sharp   glinting Mica,
Feldspar tumbled over milk-pink quartz,
Enough to make the summer sunlight ache—

Hovers…then down past draughty caverns
Vastly ancient, twisting about itself
In columns solid with an evanescent
Play of light and flash and flesh and lift—

Defies shoulders   shudders   sheers of face-cliffs
Barely visual—to plunge ecstatic
Cold and boiling into substance cleft
And cloven   woven with all-shades of life—

Into the ceaseless blue of silent music…
Calmly warming   blue-lit   cool mosaic

* * * * *

  The first step, in carrying out the Great Plan, was to secure a place on which the desired experience might be gained. To accomplish this, the earth was made from materials found in the universe, which, by the intelligent power of God, were collected and organized into the earth. [John A. Widtsoe 45]

Fog, Like Snow

   frosts arid chaparral   mottled ce-
anothus crowns submerge   nearby ridge-flanks
age   lighten   disappear   one by one days
mutely slide unneeded as slick fog banks
forward huddles reverses to grey seas

each day fog ingests one bite more   quests a
moment longer   wraps one more distant ridge
denying shadow   spreading softened shapes
woolly-wrapped in cotton-fog   white-spun fog
sparkled with facet drops dependent from
slick-smooth leaves   ceanothus mocks holly
dust-green shimmers scrubbed   fire-mantle-scrim
haven-bar spread beneath sun-frozen flames—
moist fog rests cool upon dry mountain breasts

* * * * *

The earth was not made from nothing, nor by the fiat of God, except as his will and words determined that the work should be undertaken. In the clumsy way of man, by adding stone to stone or material to material, the earth was not made…. [John A. Widtsoe 45]

SandStone

          —sand-and-banded-stone mottled-blood-
engorged-forging-thrusting-skyward pinnacle
mud-and-blood-pressured-stone tower cold-
ly wearing iron weight of   years   nipping

wind-tears   cracking pins of elemental
ice   burst infinitesimal frac-
tures   wedge submicroscopic molecules—
moisture waging immortal war with mock-

ing grit […] scouring wind […] blistering
sun— molecules wedge   freeze   expand   fall
heat on heat   gristly   gritty   sledge bearing
drop-wedging   shards break   fragmental fila-

ment shudders   separates a hairbreadth crack
topples monoliths to   waiting   grating rock

* * * * *

....[R]ather, great forces, existing in the universe, and set into ceaseless operation by the directing intelligence of God, assembled and brought into place the materials constituting the earth, until, in the course of long periods of time, this sphere was fitted for the abode of man. [John A. Widtsoe 45]

Seashallows

seashallows dance chrome-indigo   life-sear-
ing sun eclipsed   its balled-up shroud a pall
of crumpled black   crepe-rape   along a tear-
strained horizon above/beyond wave-walls
that hover-tremble-heave-themselves erect

vagrant moon gone too, dead whiteface hidden
beneath turquoise tumults   ridge-edge-ledge   backed
wave on wave shimmers upward-grasping lead
froth-plait damp
                      voyeur stars dare not condescend
to peek, to peep and pry   calm nakedness
transforms sheer ocean into leagues of bend-
ing-writhing-twisting-arcing-curling massed

musculature breaking on land-sand coves
and still seashallows dance chrome-indigo

* * * * *

The elements of all these properties or things are eternal, uncreated, self existing. Not one particle can be added to them by creative power. Neither can one particle be diminished or annihilated.[Parley P. Pratt 50]

Rain

—and the backyard a grizzle-bearded
wild of lush-tufted weeds   love-knot-twined ger-
aniums peek through dust   crocuses rear
toward pocked canopies   apples plump bare
twigs with wooden buds   peaches and apri-
cots little more than lint-brush green   from dim
dark the next stray storm-cloud gathers steel-dry
curves against sunset-glare
                                         Tomorrow when
incipient grass strains high   hard peach-pods
tangle bluff and moist   crocuses spike slow
thick sticky heads to counter thirst   rain-beat-
en breeze-blown apple branches swing and nod
solemn deference to spring   I shall mow
and trim and thin   preparing for the heat

*****

    In the making of the earth, as in all other matters pertaining to the destiny of man, the work was done in complete and orderly harmony with the existing laws of the universe. The forces of nature act steadily but slowly in the accomplishment of great works. [John A. Widtsoe 45]

Thistles

Along prim pasture-rows random thistles
root to haunt dim musty memories in
airless torpid pungent afternoons   Sessile
topknot-shoots tuft volcanic-stagnant flame
Cool lava spurts cloud-light ash-thick into
unstirring air   floats motionless an instant
settles in a pregnant wash of fiber

on grey-green-dusty waiting milkweed cups

Volatile   threatening thistles nettle-warn
wayward cows that graze toward the west
Unassaulted crowns of purple crest
low pastures   until stiff summer's age warms
flame to subtle snows that—patient—wait....
In harvest winds drift-thistles abdicate

* * * * *

    Yet, surely, there will be a tomorrow. The sun sets, and we sleep, and we awaken to a new day. Forever there shall come new days. Today is our great day; but there will be another great, a greater day. What tomorrow shall be depends measurably upon today. At least, the beginning of tomorrow will be as the evening of today. As we spend today, so will the hope of tomorrow be. The ages do not come in leaps, but step by step do they enter into the larger life.

    The law of today is that joy will transfigure each coming tomorrow if our work be well done today. No man knows whether his tomorrow will be on this earth or in another existence, with new duties and under a new environment. Of one thing we are sure, beyond all cavil, that life on earth will continue into an endless future, and the work will be taken up where it was laid down yesterday. [John A. Widtsoe 171]

* * * * *

Gwyn Tour

    -beast slipping//sleeping   over all
white-glint fall to cancel columned greens and
sheen instead in cold-fire harmony   Pal-

try thirst first scattered by a miser's hand

White-tower-beast sleeping//creeping   soft mounds
enfold sharp crystalline fangs consum-
ing//inhuming   above white-flight redounds
hangs silhouette against a thrice-howled moon

Wyntour-beast creeping//heaping leaving no-
track no-trace no-hibernation-place
no-grace inter-froze between steep foe
and waiting grating white-beast-buried face

Winter-beast heaping//weeping   anticipat-
ing   dissipating   baiting   verdant fate

* * * * *

    I wish here to ask our young friends as well as the older ones, the question: Do you ever consider or contemplate anything about the number of evil spirits that occupy the earth, who are at war against God and all good, and who seek to destroy all the children of men in every age of the world?
    .... We will suppose that there were 100,000,000,000 of fallen spirits sent down from heaven to earth, and that there are, 1,000,000,000 of inhabitants upon the face of the earth to-day, that would make one hundred evil spirits to every man, woman, and child living on the earth; and the whole mission and labor of these spirits is to lead all the children of men to do evil and to effect their destruction. [Wilford Woodruff, 83, 84]

A Stalker's Sonet

Now I have seen your calmness. Shake and crack
As you might wish me to, I have seen.

I promised yesterday I would come back
To visit you…to give you what you lack—.

I've watched. I've seen your calmness shake and crack
Like cliff-slides after torrent-squalls. I've been
Where passion engulfs all in muddy black—
I promised yesterday I would come back….

Yes, I will come—I know the subtle knack
In the *NO*-s you speak and the *YES*-es you mean,
Sense better than yourself can know your wrack
And heat. I've seen your calmness shake and crack…..

I will return—engulf you as my Queen
In Blood in caustic fragrance copper-keen.

Minotaur [II]

Through labyrinthine *NewYorkLosAngelesChicago* weaves Beast<small>MAN</small>/Man<small>BEAST</small>   sexual Hunger feeds pain with <small>PAIN</small> with P<small>AIN</small>

She walks highheeled knitting shadow-next-shadowed bled-threads of passing   knitting moment to bleak moment   falters beneath a streetlamp   sparse light spilling from soiled globes that barely shadow   falters   glances back clutches purple-sequined purse   slips into shadow   screams   pain for <small>PAIN</small> for P<small>AIN</small> he feeds sates sexuality   Man<small>BEAST</small>—head and genitals of man   heart/soul of beast

Unraveling patterns in *NewYork Los AngeleslabyrinthineChicago*

* * * * *

> By the knowledge of opposites, man may draw conclusions of far-reaching importance in his course of progression. The operations of the devil and his powers may, therefore, serve some good in giving contrasts for man's guidance. This does not mean that it is necessary for man to accept the suggestions of the evil one, or to commit evil to know truth. On the contrary, every rational impulse resents the thought that a man must know sin so that he may know righteousness better. Unfortunately, the works of the evil one may be plentifully observed in the world, among those who have forsaken the Great Plan and the path of progression. [John A. Widtsoe 81]

NY/LA Any Moment/Any Day

sulfur-scented serpents   hooded chlorine
cobras coil/swirl/coil solid cornices
concrete-flicking gargoyle-tongues twisting fangs
to reeling steely skies   threadhaze venoms trespass
around her stony head   twine sinuous
swerve   carve   shear spatter score aluminum
planes   abrade cold glass   lest Perseus
attempt to slay by mirror-sheer reflection

stone grimaces   dread poisoned approach/touch
chill as scales scratch granite-marble-lime corrode
reduce to elemental dust   black dust
rust dust grey ceremental dust   abrade
old nameless saints   gryphons   gargoyles grin-gash-
mouthed grind earthbone stone   batter blackened ash

On Seeing the Unretouched Original of a Bowdlerized Nineteenth Century Anthropological Photograph

he stares   she twists to/ward him   one naked
breast couched in-[ribcage]-curve   smooth mahogan-
y [one presumes]   he stares straight/strait a head
un twisted un disturbed by alien
presence urging stillness little self-soul's-
death   slow thickness de scends unconcerned un
clothed unhid den [later scratches artful-
ly rape the plate, ironic focus on
what is no longer there]   her fullness coils
overlap-ping shells   echo-ing sep-
ia shells overneck betweenbreasts   swells
endlessly   breastbellythigh   arc of foot
they nakednudeunclothed shame timevoyeurs
be-hind/be-neath fibrous glossy burdens

Countdown—Thirteen Hours Gone... Thirty-Five to Go
18 March 2003

Forty years ago—noon-blackened skies
Over John Barrett Elementary.
The sun hung, a diminished, tarnished dime
Hidden in flat sheathes of floating ash.
Hot air, heavy with flames a hundred miles
Away, breath-aching still, sedentary....
Stark pupils peered uneasily through webbed-
Wire glass at midday darkness, eyes awash
With acrid stinging. For the moment, lights
Switched on, closed windows locked—cautionary,
To protect the students. All might have passed
In eerie, silent night...had not the gash
Of terror echoed through corridors, cries

That ripped the stillness…incendiary
Cries more startling than the black flat crisp-sheet
Of sky.
    "The end of the world!"
                              She splashed
Daubs of sound as she whirled once, night-laced eyes
Staring-white, cheeks ash-white, face white-scary-
Stiff—she screamed into the sepulchre
Our room had suddenly become…then dashed
Beyond sight, into darkness, wild surprise
Warbling after her. Some stifled wary
Gasps; other mouths hiccoughed softly into
Cupped hands. Somewhere, her strident voice crashed
Against rough concrete walls, rose, wailed, and died.
Blackness melted from the sky to bury
Barrett in haunting residues of flames.
Ash etched reddened eyes with prickling flashes.

Today…the East threatens flat, blackened skies.
"The end of the world!" howls, scrawled in ashes

Dance of the Post-Millennial Hours

some taunt, scratch, absently scrawl blue-bled lines.
some—red-rimed eyed—shift sandaled, curled feet,
thrust telepathic earthquake jitter-tines,
convulse sublunary worlds in magma-heat.
some grin and greet fear-distant silent spheres,
those left before and those behind. but some
intimidate …. not threat…not dare…not sneer…
but twist—hint—turn corroded khaki bone
at crotch distended by a searching hand
stripe white then slump…then crude
image-thought irresolute, shun/stunned,
devolve to furtive shadow-echo-words—
deeper, wider, darker vortices where loom

passions to pattern, swallow, and consume.

* * * * *

When the planet on which he dwells has conceived, brought forth and nourished the number of tabernacles assigned to it in its rudimental state, by infinite wisdom, it must needs be acted upon by a chemical process. The purifying elements, for instance, fire, must needs be employed to bring it through an ordeal, a refinement, a purification, a change commensurate with that which had before taken place in the physical tabernacle of its inhabitants…. [Parley P. Pratt 61]

Fifth Movement...And Final
Symphony in E-Minor "From the New Worlds"
[Organ Transcription]
Second Recension

sound shudders   console cramps beneath twisted barbs   molten flesh fencing with pinioned flutes—
mourning doves stutter ruddy lines of fate cathedral/calm   storm-fires rubyFires through stone/lattice   ruby-shivered-glass shards stone-bone floors

                    I play
                            GhostChoir antiphonies
nave   birth/death at one   I   orchestrating darkness   bloodLight oozes on thick ivory

sound shudders   organ weeps ultimate music penultimate.
I the last

black/captive notes   beyond whiteAsh gray/Looming wreak/wreck/wrack world   petulant defile

Fifth Movement   Syn/Symphony uncomposed—
Climax thrusting into deepest *oneliness*

* * * * *

 Thus renovated, it is adapted to resurrected man.
[Parley P. Pratt 61]

Desiccated Flame

Desiccated flame encrusts the rock
The air   the very breath that labors
Its harsh lungs taught tight strait   dry-fire rakes
All essence to a leaden heap…embers

Beyond remembery   sublimated
Adust   golden melancholy touching
Essence with its grimly cessant motion
Infusing   effusing   refusing beseechings

To longer linger, finger with deft
Sanguine touch face of rock and shade and earth
Until inexorable gravity wafts
Spinning motes   into the throat of glory-birth

Where irrigated flames consume the dust…
And All reveals through shimmer-sentient mist

* * * * *

 The curse, so-called, pronounced by God upon Adam as he went out of the Garden of Eden, that in the sweat of his brow he should earn his bread, is possibly the greatest of all human blessings, and it is a simple extension of another great eternal law. From the beginning of the dim past, when man slumbered with only a feeble thought of his possible vast future, the compelling law of progress has been that only personal effort can achieve desirable things. The price to be paid for advancement is vigorous self-effort. The active will precedes every step of progress. To exercise the will means labor, which may well be represented by 'the sweat of the brow.' [John A. Widtsoe 47-48]

LiveOak

Writhe-oak live-oak wraith-wreath stark against a dark-
Blue plum-bruise sky   *Götterdämmerung*
In bare-branch black   Druidic as mute murky
Tarns that once pronounced dire mysteries among
Bruit-pagan forebears
                    Stark still against
Black cut-out sky   made real by outlined
Absent stars obscured inferred sea-sand dense
Except where live-oaks tentacle tendril
Then and now
          At dawn   grey-dusky green
Musty even in beginning light   dagger-
Digits gnarl against the coming sheen
Curl and twist   whorl resist-less jagged-

Ragged leaves   pin-prickling breezes gaunt
Invade dark live-oaks   writhe-oaks   wraiths and haunts

Sonata Contorta

In nakedness nests biting truth, tightly
Wrapped upon itself in writhing balls
Of infant rattlesnakes new-hatched and curled
Against cold nights in echoing midnight rooms.
    Truth lies quiescent, warming, coiling—strikes,
Floods flaming poison into veins, devours

Systematically too thin tissue-lies
Constructed to objectify our blame.
   Truth viper-strikes through bitter nakedness,
Limns stomach, thigh, breast, and arm—guileless, blunt,
Exposing wrinkled age and youth-heat's waste
As we lie darkly, staring into dark.
   In nakedness nests truth, alone, poised
   To poison-cleanse dim lives close-nights have soiled.

* * * * *

   .... All elements of the material universe are eternal.

   ....There is a divine substance, fluid or essence, called spirit, widely diffused among these eternal elements.

   This spiritual substance is the most refined, subtle and powerful element in the universe. It is endowed with all wisdom, all intelligence and power. In short, it is the light, life, power and principle of all things by which they move, and of all intelligences by which they think.

   This divine element, or spirit, is the immediate active or controlling agent in all holy miraculous powers. [Parley P. Pratt 100]

GodFinger

GodFinger rakes ragged tags of blue-
still-peace   white-curling over white until
it shoals time-encrusted   collapsing time-hewn
grit-made-stone   embraces crushes into   lull

[From where I stand upon the cliff, the moment
Hesitates, my gaze drops, greets the wind's; and
Sand and sea and cliff and Face-of-God combine

Into their single startling element
That shares equally of breath and glint, land
And fluid intricately entwined...]

far off   GodFinger begins again again
Infinitely roils   spiraling gestation
Toward new shoalings   liberated grains
Condense again   again   into Creation

* * * * *

> The orderly cosmos is the product of divine powers acting through ordained laws upon eternal elements that possess certain innate and acquired properties of life or intelligence. The elements are able to respond to the will of God in such a way that they are sustained in their respective spheres of existence. Consequently, the universe is a living, moving system, not a static, stationary one. [Hyrum L. Andrus, 157]

Eagle

entity of earth and water   wooden
flight   straining to at-one with air   with fire—
feather   beak   and claw poised over hot blood
turgid earth-blood scorching pinnacle/lair

mail-linked feathered head glacier-pale eyes
not-white/not-blue translucent glare/stare/dare-
ing   eight-foot wingspan arched/stretched/arced essays/
conspires/aspires to ascend   beyond bare

stark-laced granite shoulders   barren pine-knot
tops burdened with two thousand pounds of nest-
ling twigs/branches/moss   earth-dead plant-nest that
flings wings   outward upward skyward   air-crest

outline dark against cerulean   light
curving up-/out-/skyward   coveting flight

* * * * *

    An immortal man, possessing a perfect organization of spirit, flesh, and bones, and perfected in his attributes, in all the fullness of celestial glory, is called a God.
    An immortal man, in progress of perfection, or quickened with a lesser degree of glory, is called an Angel.
    An immortal spirit of man, not united with a fleshly tabernacle, is called a Spirit.
    An immortal spirit, clothed with a mortal tabernacle, is called a Man. [Parley P. Pratt, 42]

Greenery

swollen with potentiality of seed
[*potens, potere*, 'to be able', 'to
have power'—dim shadow-word from long-dead
Latin]   the green ignites underneath a

summer-sun   explosive bursts of green
hand-breadth wide and thick/thin lush as taste
hover as if with pinioned angel-wings
over branch and trunk and root   arms out-stretch

silk-haloed in shrill heat   shadows march their
order over man-earth-ribs rippling with
fecund growth   summer's burgeoning share
of elemental *virtu* strains to birth

shaggy garments fade to naked strength
and greening verdure preens through day-shine's length

* * * * *

    The question is often asked, "Does nature, as we know it, the rocks and trees and beasts, possess intelligence of an order akin to that of man?" Who knows? That intelligence is everywhere present is beyond question. By an intelligent God nature is directed. The forming of a crystal or the conception of a living animal is, somehow, connected with an intelligent purpose and will….

    The earth as an organism does its work perfectly well. It is without sin. [John A. Widtsoe 155-156]

Creekrock

creekrock sleek-rock ticking geoLogic
time   cold-moss-hung clock-intrusion fractured
cutting/jutting/rutting iced-magmatic
tears glacial tears condensed coarse-crystal hard-

ness   thrusting/bursting/thirsting   melting heat
compression into quartz   feldspar [pink-white
plagioclase sheer orthoclase] grain-grat-
ing crush crystal into crystal into light

softness melts hardness endures inures it-
self to aeons   weight pressure heat   heat
pressure weight   and shatters with unending bite
ice snow wind heat snow Wind Ice Time   abate

weight   thick-sediment-clothing slides away
creekrock glistens moistens   enlightens day

* * * * *

Let us turn from the contemplation of scenes so sublimely fearful. Suffice it to say, the mandate came, darkness fled, the veil was lifted, light pierced the gloom, and chaos was made visible. O what a scene! A world without landscape, without vegetation, without animal life, without man or animated beings. No sound broke on the stillness, save the voice of the moaning winds and of dashing, foaming waters. Again, a voice comes booming over the abyss, and echoing amid the wastes, the mass of matter hears and trembles, and lo! the sea retires, the muddy, shapeless mass lifts its head above the waters. Molehills to mountains grow. huge islands appear, and continents at length expand to view, with hill and vale, in one wide, dreary waste, unmeasured and untrodden. [Parley P. Pratt 54]

Console

"Organ playing is the manifestation of a will intent upon Eternity."
—Charles-Marie Widor

Michel/Angel's wrenched half-captive nudes
emergent-/surgent-/urgent-ly press flesh
flushed pillar-bone   pallid muscle   raw-rude
rich   blood-flood-sculpted tissue   breathing   h u s h

thin hidden slatted-captives skirt slack screens—
heathen/pagan agonists twist hell/shell
torsos tight/taut   pocked wrists flick   neck-arcs scream
exultations   r i s e   retreat   entrench   s w e l l

forefront captives   naked   ward all Vision
to themselves   forefront frontal barricade
throat rote/tight   knot-clot adam's-ripple sheen
solid/stolid foundation-pipe   fluting   GREAT-

ness outward   wretched/wrenched half-captives nude-echo-songs engulf bronze-black imprisoned hood

* * * * *

It is the image of the descending stars to which I draw attention, for the correct and conventional way of designating holy persons who descend to earth to carry out assignments among men is to call them stars, or the stars that shine above the stars. [Hugh Nibley 228]

On a Display of Swordsmanship

Toes flat-tensed on drab commercial-grade
Celedon, in jeans and T you swing
blue steel—hook sharp fingers as if to rape
raw blighted stars ricketing in pain—
forearm hedgerow-tendons flail to harvest
rebel blood—flash from field to grave between
heartbreath beats. ***   Silent silver weaves its
artifice of light, conjures Babylon,
Ur, Egypt's dust-hagged Magic—warriors' arms
quivering beneath dead weight—brass, iron,
electrum's silver-gold brash against far-
rising suns—heaving, brittle, hack-hewn lungs—
pummel naked everlasting Glory
beneath the dust of frigid Harmony.

Predator

shoulder-ember   Arab-named intensity
a thousand multiples of yellow suns—
red-swollen massy vast immensity
five hundred years beyond light's quick-shrug run

ankle eye-of-god-bright light   blue-white-on-
white   titanic glow five-thousand tens more
luminous than ancient-yellow sparking wanes—
nine hundred years beyond our light-fleshed core

static water   frozen sword-tip   barely
flare of night   bright hesitance half-spun be-
tween cock-surely-seen   feigned-unseen-surely-
known   spot/blue/wheeling   milk-sheen/circled/worlds

Alnitak/Mintaka/Alnilam— belt
of potence   harness-glow celestial

* * * * *

    The earth and other systems are to undergo a variety of changes in their progress towards perfections. Water, fire, and other elements are the agents of these changes. But it is an eternal, unchangeable fact, a fixed law of nature, easily demonstrated by chemical experiment, that neither fire nor any other element can annihilate a particle of matter, to say nothing of a whole globe. [Parley P. Pratt, 60]

Blood Rite

It's serious, they say—National Psych-
iatric Guild-certified, AMA-
-verified, God only knows how many
others have bothered themselves, probed and poked
ones like me. It's serious—true—but all
I know is that sweet, waiting pain when I
scrape blunt nails (pared to one ragged edge) a-
long the nape of crisp-dried blood. I revel
in sharp tug of nail on clotted scab, lift-
ing a brittle edge, pulling harder, then
the brightness swells beneath, red pulsing wedge

of unsheathed flame. I scrape again, unfet-
tering the flow…and watch it pool furrows
in pleasing, random patterns—see it catch
white-ridged scars and fresh, still-tender welts…watch,
mesmerized. I smell warm blood-scent, harrow
lips to back of hand—salty self emerges,
tongue to skin—completes dark, secret urges.

Night

bruise-blue-black counter-element anti-
element, unLight disembodied   drapes
dark as skeleton branches hang at eve-
ning in bleak December   bruise-black shape

antithesis of form   leafless starkness
darkness invades sky tree rock stone   all Earth
all Air   all Sea   all Flame   transmuted flesh
of dayShine forced against/into itself

antagonist of light   agonistic
day contracts against *in*equinox   ex-
pands // contracts / / expands   and severs vatic
silence   heals bruise-black neon-glow and nox-

ious night drapes the rood-arm-cross of mourning
remnant of the struggle to be born

* * * * *

    God, exalted by his glorious intelligence, is moving on into new fields of power with a rapidity of which we can have no conception, whereas man, in a lower stage of development, moves relatively at a snail-like, though increasing pace. Nevertheless, man is moving onward in eternal progression. "As man is, God once was; as God is, man may become." In short, man is a god in embryo. He comes of a race of gods, and as his eternal growth is continued, he will approach more nearly the point which to us is Godhood, and which is everlasting in its power over the elements of the universe. [John A. Widtsoe, 25]

Silently, as with a Blade-Edge, We Sever our Respective Silences: For a Grand-Daughter

we commune then she and I in some dis-
tant place where petals peek through shyness where they
tongue proud consonants and sleek soft vowels
where cloudbanks *humm* incessant melody

distilled as tears when earth becomes too dry
but sucks with infant eagerness at buds
we commune then she and I with eye and eye-
lids shuttering in well-content sleep's nod

with touch to touch, her finger-lengths enclosed
broadside on mine and not enough not yet
but soon as soon as whirlwinds that flood
prime petals to awaiting ear that send

again sublunar notes up to the moon
and then o then shall she and I commune

Music of the Spheres

Earth—Air— Water   Flame—
Fire falling from crystalline Outer Sphere—

Sphere of God—down to Earth-Dust-World
World where we are second-born—

On its way—pure-poured Flame vibrating Sun—
Moon—Stars—Wanderers through blue Night—

Flame touches incandescent eternals—
Spirits of Fire eager for breath and dust—

Eager to descend concentric Spheres—
Become one with Earth—pass through Water—

Ascend Air—rejoin the Fount of All-Flame—
Elemental Unity at the End of All—

Unity—Infinity—Eternity—
Earth—Air—Fire—Water…Children of Highest God ….

* * * * *

It appears at the commencement of this grand work, that the elements, which are now so beautifully arranged and adapted to vegetable and animal life, were found in a state of chaos, entirely unadapted to the uses they now serve.

There was one vast mixture of elements. Earth, water, soil, atmosphere—in short, the entire elements of which this mass was composed seem to have been completely compounded or mingled into one vast chaos, and the whole overwhelmed with a darkness so dense as to obscure the light of heaven. [Parley P. Pratt 54]

Filling the measure of his responsibilities in the world of spirits, he passes by means of the resurrection of the body, into his fourth estate or sphere of human existence. In this sphere he finds himself clothed upon with an eternal body of flesh and bones, with every sense and every organ restored and adapted to their proper use. He is thus prepared with organs and faculties adapted to the possession and enjoyment of every element of the physical or spiritual worlds, which can gratify the senses or conduce to the happiness of intelligences. He associated, converses, loves, thinks, acts, moves, sees, hears, tastes, smells, eats, drinks and possesses.

In short, all the elements necessary to his happiness, being purified, exalted and adapted to the sphere in which he exists, are placed within his lawful reach, and made subservient to his use. [Parley P. Pratt 58]

Author's Afterword

What in the World—Any World!—Is This Fellow Up To?

Allusive.
Elusive.
Illusive.

In their own ways, these words suggest something of the power I hoped to embed within each of the Elementals. And each suggests something of the genesis of the poems as individuals and as a coherent—or perhaps incoherent—sequence.

Tracking down where poems come from is always simultaneously fascinating and frustrating, rewarding and surprising. The Elementals have perhaps the most complex genealogy of any literary form I have yet attempted, deriving from several sources extending back some thirty years. On the surface, they seem an immediate outgrowth of the two "Remembery" sequences previously published in *Ygdrasil* (April 1996, August 1998). Those two sequences adapted the sonnet as form to autobiography as subject, manipulating the former to lend poetic unity and (I hope) interest to the latter. In the process of exploring instants of memory, at least partially in order to understand the strands of influence that constitute a full life, I discovered how malleable the sonnet form could be. As *Remembery* progressed, I tried to strain all of the criteria for sonnets to their limit: iambic pentameter gave way to syllabics, generally nine to eleven syllables per line; perfect rhyme gave way to slanting rhyme, to half rhyme, to echoic rhyme; neat quatrains and couplets found themselves shifting, weaving, blending in strange ways. The results seemed to be sonnets that were not quite sonnets, poems that sounded as much like colloquial speech as poetry, autobiographical instants that expanded to incorporate an entire life.

And there the experiment with form would end.

I thought.

Even as I wrote the final *Remembery* poems, however, something even more radical began to suggest itself in my poetry. What if more than form—rhythm, rhyme, structure—were pushed to its limits? What if language itself—spelling, punctuation, typography, spacing—were also pushed to the extremes, then coupled with content that was itself self-reductive, struggling to understand essences…all captured in something that retained the outlines of the sonnet, perhaps the most elegantly refined and certainly among the most historically traditional of all English verse forms?

What if the poems became captured instants that in turn attempted to capture universals?

The next logical step was to identify precisely what kind of 'universals'—'elementals'—I wanted to explore. And here, another strand became critical. Since long before my formal graduate studies in Renaissance literature, I have been fascinated by sixteenth-and seventeenth-century English literature, history, culture, society, and life. A late high-school infatuation with Milton and *Paradise Lost* resulted in an eighteen-month flirtation with Renaissance epic…and twenty-five years later with the final version of a twelve-book Renaissance epic, *The Nephiad*. A separate but related project in constructing a time-line of the seventeenth-century resulted in a closer understanding of the essentially *visual* nature of Renaissance thought. And my traumatic exposure to chemistry in high school was still vivid enough in memory to assure me that I was neither capable of nor interested in examining *elements* in the modern sense.

So, in keeping with reductive sense of the poems themselves, I moved backwards.

>Earth, Air, Fire, Water—the elements separating themselves from chaos. Chaos evolving into increasingly complex and sophisticated spheres of order. Order expanding to fill the cosmos. Cosmos… well, at

that point, not even poetry would be sufficient to say what would have to be said.

Thus the Elementals came into being. Highly structured and ordered, in spite of surface appearances, they struggle to restrain chaos into order, order into cosmos, and cosmos into eternity. While remaining poems. And existing as self-contained moments of poetic expression.

Perhaps no poet is ever quite certain that the results of imagination touch reality precisely as hoped. I read the Elementals and see not only their words and pictures but the entire flow of imagination that went into their creation. Readers must take on faith that there are pathways leading from apparent point A to apparent point Z; those pathways are imprinted indelibly upon my memory. But to some extent, the Elementals seem to have succeeded as I intended.

Shortly after completing the typescript for the sequence, I asked a colleague and fellow-poet at Pepperdine University to read it and comment it. His responses were gratifying:

> I very much enjoyed reading your earth, air, fire, water sonnet sequence. What a nice combination of physics and poetry, and what an intriguing form. They strike me as elemental, nuclear-fused sonnets, free radicals one electron away from exploding.... To use Poe's phrase, you are both poet and mathematician.

While I appreciated the implicit praise, I appreciated even more the descriptive phrasing: "nuclear-fused sonnets, free radicals one electron away from exploding."

Precisely what I had hoped.

Now, of course, the Elementals must stand on their own. I can talk as long as I wish (overly long, perhaps) about what I *wanted* to happen. I can quote a fellow-poet about what *he* perceived. But ultimately, the Elementals—as do all things elemental—must remain free to combine with other minds and other imaginations, to *illude, elude*, and *allude* according to their own generative power.

A BANQUET OF SONETS

A Banquet of Sonets

Foreword

While a number of the following poems were originally conceived as extensions of earlier sonnet-series—especially *Remembery, Taliesin,* and *Elemental Sonets* (initial versions of which all appeared as issues of *Ygdrasil*), I found myself hesitant to add them or to print new editions of the earlier series.

Instead, it seemed as if at least part of me was beginning to view these poems, as varied in content and theme as they were, as part of something new. They expanded on old thoughts and images, perhaps, and certainly exploring further the potentials of the form—the 'fragmented sonets'—that has preoccupied me now for nearly a decade; but somehow they defied all attempts to allow them to settle quietly (and quiescently) into old series.

Then serendipitously (as so many things are in the world of words-as-art), while reading backgrounds for a class to be taught this fall, I came upon the following passage relating to George Chapman's Elizabethan poem, *The Banquet of the Senses*:

> Ficino, in his commentary on Plato's *Banquet (Symposium)* had arranged the five senses in order, below the power of reason: sight, hearing, smell, taste, touch. Touch was the most earthly of the five, because it depended most on physical contact. Sight was the most spiritual, because no physical contact was necessary. The senses were regarded by Ficino as steps on the ladder to rational apprehension. Two years after the publication of [Shakespeare's] *Venus and Adonis* Chapman brought out his *Ovid's Banquet of Sense,* a poem which can be read as an adverse commentary on Shakespeare's poem. It is notoriously obscure and difficult, even among Chapman's works, but it is capable of interpretation. Chapman at least provided an

Argument, in which he informs the reader that Ovid, newly enamoured of (Augustus's daughter) Julia, whom he calls Corinna, is led on from hearing her singing to the lute, through the senses of smell, sight, and taste, 'to entreaty for the fifth sense and there is interrupted'. This scheme, which is the Ficinian scheme used by Shakespeare, is mixed up in Chapman's poem with another, that of the Five Lines of Love, and there is a counterpoint between the two motifs. This second scheme derives from Donatus' commentary on a passage in Terence's *Eunuchus*: 'Quinque lineae perfectae sunt ad amorem: prima visus; secunda loqui; tertia tactus; quarta osculari; quinta coitus'; sight, conversation, touching, kissing, coition. In the poem Ovid sophistically defends the banquet of the senses (which is implicitly opposed to the Platonic, or Ficinian, scheme) for its own sake. He uses much learning to prove that the progress of love is, so to say, down the ladder. But surely Chapman is being ironical.... (Buxton, 301)

For a moment, I paused, trying to visualize the connections between poetry and these once-current psychologies/philosophies of the senses...until, with something akin to amazement, I realized that *here* was the organizing principle underlying all of these new poems.

The general movement was not particularly new. *Elemental Sonets* had been based on movement downward and upward—from Macrocosm to Microcosm (Earth) and back again, with a healthy dash of late Renaissance chemistry of the Four Elements. And most of my poetry (so I have been told) is highly sense-oriented, focusing as it frequently does upon the natural world.

It then remained simply to arrange the poems, from the most elevated and ethereal—those corresponding to sight—to the most physical and troubling—those related touch. The arrangement is not perfect; nor was it intended to be. Several poems might have fit as neatly in another category as in the ones in which they finally appear. There is no attempt at symmetry among the parts of the series, just as our senses do not impinge upon us with equal intensity. In spite of these decisions, the poems do seem to hang together. They are all sonnets—or, to remain true to my sixteenth-century originals, *Sonets*.[4] Most have fourteen lines, but some may have more or fewer. Most have a rough rhyme scheme, but some may depend heavily upon slant rhyme while others may suggest free verse. Many have an underlying iambic beat, but some consciously attempt to subvert that beat and replace it with alternate ways of creating rhythm. And, like to many of the Elizabethan sonnets, many sound autobiographical; but all—even those triggered by a memory or a moment from my life—have been shaped, formed, and arranged beyond the boundaries of autobiography and, I hope, into something near art.

---

4. This unusual spelling was suggested by the title of Richard Tottel's *Songess and Sonettes*, written by the ryght honorable Lorde Henry Haward late Earle of Surrey, and other (1557), which its more familiar nonce-title, Tottel's *Miscellany*, was among the most influential source-books for the later Elizabethan poets. A generation later, John Donne echoed Tottel with his own *Songs and Sonets*, of which, scholars have noted, not a single one fits our contemporary definition of 'sonnet.' Since the 16th century did not limits its conception of the sonnet to a 14-line poem in iambic pentameter, with an unvarying rhyme scheme, neither have I.

A Banquet of Sonets

Exotica—Elemental Sonet

Long and lean—sole curvature against
A panoply of blues—cerulean
Cobalt with subtle hints of cerise
Where sunlight glints and slides—long and lean

In sunbaked brown—monotonously
Rich complexly umber—enough to crown
Sensations in silkworn sands—lushly
Sterile emptiness— —a single mound

Rides midway visible—rioting
Citrine—amethyst—sapphire—emerald—
Gemrich palmfronds—blossoms uniting
Heat and moisture—desert arable

Swirls of bracken—honeycombed moss—
Dew-parched petioles—silent loss

Hæmatite

eagle-flight   light-/height-/flight-ed fantasy
azure/pleasure   leisure-feather-lilted
shifting cloudbanks   shifting ice-crushed Ecstasy
upward soaring flaring faring   jilted-

jolted-folded earthward   wingSinging harsh
airbursts fragmentary EchoSong   long
lost now   glossed now to mere memory   brash
flash/slash of eagle-gray suspended   hung

breath-length eye-blink   then sinking further/farther

Azure transmogrified as SilverBlack
flecks of fire/heat/blood   condensed-ice ardor
frailing dream/scream of flight   in   crystalled slack

crimson-crystalled water weeps FloodMoans—
weeps and wets   glints/cuts/abrades BloodStone

* * * * *

THE SENSES

Tinnitus

I sit to write a sonnet—*sssssssssssssssssss*—a
Sonnets*ssssssssssssssssss*sonnet and words
refuse, ducking beneath a stuttering, cluttering
ghost that hags my neural channels*sssssssssss*
clots thoughts and crackles—*crackcrackcrack*—
raises mental hackles and the poem that
was to be dissipates*sssssssssssssssssss* I wrack
and rend, curse, weep, contend—*buzzzzzzzzzz*—

I sit to—small nails in glass swirling tinkling
chinking tinkling—sit to write a sssssssssss
sssssssssssssss—PAUSE. BREATHE. PAUSE.
Mozart? *ssssssss* MozArt?—*ring*was that the tele
gggggggggggggggggggggggggggg—God!
{no imprecation but a prayer}

Tinnitus—At the Organ

They sit behind the organ, whispering—
not reverent, no—but neither are they rude-
ly speaking—voices low-pitched, barely carry-
ing to waiting rows of wooden pews.

They sit behind me, whispering—it should
not make a difference as I play—I'm lost
in notes that once would flow into a prelude
to the worship-mood I hope to cast....

And now do not—their late-adolescent
basses grate across sharp tenors in
my ears, my mind, my brain—their nascent
conversations dim the glory of brass
pipes—intrude between the music and my
soul—and trigger mindless anger as I play.

On Seeing Photographs of
My Grandfather in His Middle-Age

He floats unfinished, elemental—cheeks
Stubble-rough with whitened whiskers, hair
Wildly corn-shock coarse and peppered black
On white, lips thin and quavering and quer-
-ulous with looming age. Even—rarely—when
I see him young, ambitious, smooth, largely,
Eager to consume the world; then
Or later, hearth-black-tincted by his forge,
Leather apron glossy in the heat;
Or later still a hatted silhouette
Anonymous in the corn—even then
There is about him that which, silent, cries
For grinder, sander, lathe, and polish to
Finish incompleteness—give him life.

Glimpses

A crow's-flight-mile west from 101
(Where asphalt trails curve against spring-green
And air-borne spoor from semis, cars, and vans
Serpents willows and coiled, ash-grey ferns)—

There, still in earshot of the muted roar,
A mountain-cat startled from the lush-grass
Shadow of a hummock. It paused. It stared—
A hundred feet away—then loped across

My ragged prints to another slice of shade.
I turned aside, climbed the newly rain-wet
Firebreak to a rock-toothed crest. It stretched.
I waited, watched across knee-high wild oats,

Stood breath-locked as it stared—then fled. The last
I saw—tawny blemish blending into mist.

Mountain Hike

Alone. Embedded in densely layered
Chaparral—scrub oak, black sage, chamise,
Yucca, ceanothus—trapped in ambered
shadows, gray-green-not-gold, fringed with cerise

manzanita, I stride. The sun tints brick-
red shale to white, ripples solid-seeming
stone. Disturbing thick-scored dust, I stalk
thin-twisted serpent markings, scan teeming

Skittered quail tracks, ponder clean-drawn lines
Of lizards' tails in oppressing heat.
Alone. I stop…foot nudged…, questioning…,
Against the sand-soft spoor of a mountain cat.

I stand alone in gray-green chaparral—consumed
By sounds of wild pursuit that does not come.

Quasimodo from the Cathedral's Pinnacles:
Apollo as an Eagle

He glares at me— —arrogant hunchbacked mal-
-formed beak—talons in segmentals hung, keen
jasper roundels on raw jute—rosette bale-
-ful eyes concentric fractured shadows— —he

glares at me— —tongue protrudent like a hanged
man's taunt—skull thrust forward on pain-
-twisted neck—poised to contort, to hiss, fang-
-rage, to goad— —he urges me— —who would fain

passively devour at leisure Shakespeare's
sugar'd sonets—Milton's sharp-quilled breaths—
Wordsworth—Byron—Keats— —yet still he surges
me—and rhythms wing staccato-feather

counterpoints— —static stutters linesfeetbeats
that unexpected spring from heart-burst-heat

Jigsaw Puzzles

A hundred pieces—five hundred—once a
Thousand—in winter darkness we explored
Dutch-windmill-landscapes tainted yellow by
Unseen sunsets, age, and fading ink. Or

English gardens, thatched-roofed-shadows over
Lilac hedges blurred red-overlapping-
Blue in 3-D edges hard to focus
On. Filling borders inward, gaping

Emptiness replaced by fragment patterns
Webbing links until the picture lay
Complete. Then we might smile, her laughter

Uttering "End" to puzzle and to day.

Sometimes one missing piece—or many—kept
Us from understanding…and we slept.

Hummingbird

whisk of brown—not even breath enough
for slash of red or ruby-shimmer-green—
just whisk of brown half-sensed beyond spring-
unfurled jasmine knots—evanescent
whisper-leaves to sussurround white cream
and yellow fragrances beyond that whisk
of brown—darning in and out of naked
ligaments clinging to sketched arbors—
whisk of brown and blur of wing and sense
of arcing needle-bill searching sweetness
in bitter white-sap jasmine not yet
resigned itself to suicidal bloom
whisk of brown—whisper-sweetness-hum
on cream-and-yellow almost-jasmine home

Magpie

In drear remembery, the magpie sleeks
Beneath gray cottonwood, beneath bleak
Boxelder, beneath vined honeysuckle
Redolent with twining cream-turned-brick-
Red as double-berries crest and die;
Or in the bosky shadows that lie hedge
Beyond the outhouse, serpenting with sly-
Coiled honesty toward the pasture-edge;
Or on slick damp-gray pavers on a
Gray-sludge afternoon, between grass dark
With raindrops and moist earth lately turned—
He—gaudy-raucous—sleeks, and pseudo-speaks

Stark white-on-black as if his skreeing sound
Could surmount the misting gray surround.

Swallows

no swallows flit today DUSKYGREY be
fore a brilliant sky   bluesoblue it pains
almost—above rich CHAPARRALgreen
patchwork knotted/twisted strands of springing rain

midground—a single monarch spins slowly
dying leaf   orangeSPIRALdownward   then
aBREATHaHEAVEaSPLIT in light rolling
ORANGEtoBLACKtoORANGE in blue skyskin

foreground—smeared windowpane streaked ammoniac
smearsCHALKwhite—bleachedBONEdeadWHITE to mounds
beneath mudnests—dark mounds funerealBLACK
STUDDEDwhite monochromatic testament

to death and life   from one swollen nest by one
curled claw last year's sylphsWALLOW hangs   still   alone

Where the White Crow Flies

— Dim — dank — scum-clotted ponds breathe
Their pestilence and boil ripe contagion.
Trees— once oak or pine or yew— ease
Raddled branches to a pewter sky, grim

Arms upraised, bone-fingers retching
Ghosts of disembodied needles, leaves,
Insect-clutching galls — punkie, roach-
Infected blots of shadowed life. Stark eaves,

They overhang a dwindled earth — a soil

Barren-blasted — twitching darkness blackness
At its core. And more — ...— a distant wail —
Panicked gravity — still warns and wakens

Dead ears. A slice of light — sharded Song —
Surveying its demesne a white crow wings.

Harvest Crows

Harvest crows caw dark convocations,
Pace bone-grey walks with skeletal claws,
Haunt suburban entropy and span
Black fingers wide to polluted clay,

Waft contagion through the land. They perch upon
Rough concrete stanchions where lights once glowed at dusk,
Red-eyed, to glare deft retribution. One
Swoops and clicks and snaps diseased flesh that reeks

Beneath an August sun. Another grates
Its challenge for the filament of flesh,
Black flesh, raw flesh shimmering white against
A sable maw. And still the harvest crows press,

And congregate, and lordly strut stilt-gaunt legs
Along flat paths, asbestos drives, dead ways.

Cormorant

A single cormorant clasps a crippled face
Streaked and freaked with fading ocher stains
Where bird-lime-white once gleamed above a base
Of tumbled rock and patiently sanded grains.

The cormorant unfurls, fed by raging
Need, ragged hunger preying on its flesh—

Unfurls, rises, rides convection waves
Beyond flat swells, until its cliff-face flashes

Once and sinks. For days it rides. Scans the deeps
For shadowed signs, swoops and swirls—and nagging
Blue-harsh static sparks its neurons—ennui creeps—
Its circuit sinks   wider   lower   flagging

Until thick gray voracious ocean currents
Consume the last and final cormorant

13 Vultures

A cliché, if not by actual count
I had not seen them there—large ravens from
A distance, well fed and plump, clotted
On the fenceposts by the concrete slough

But not—no, vultures, all thirteen, heads
Scabbily bald, wattled, red-spotted,
A congregation of old men sitting
Judgment on an empty field

One clutched the barkless knurl
Of an ancient cottonwood. Another
Cut its bevel through a dustcloud raised
By cars like mine. Eleven waited

Potently on fenceposts, waited for
The corpses that must come to them.

Blackbird Fall

Beneath dark storm clouds thundering over
mountain lips, harvest-grains shrivel uncut;
lawns once placid green revert to clover;

and asphalt highways crumble into ruts.
Silence hangs. Promised brightenings hover
unfulfilled. No motion, save fluttered struts
of barren limbs. Dank prodigies cover
sightless windows lurking void and shut.

There should be children, games, kites soaring bright
skies. There should be roiling laughter. Instead,
crows and ravens plump on bitter gall,
rank starlings glitter in their sunset flight,
sable swans glide on lakes as flat as lead,
and bodies lie in state for blackbird fall.

On Speaking a Child's Blessing in November

To give a name, perpetuate a name
To look as if into a mirror's depth
And see a face and form—though not my own—
Still mine…a part of me incipient.

Sugar-maples droop red-fingered leaves to
Earth; magnolias express blood-vibrant
Drops—I speak a Blessing-Name to one whose
Breath has bloomed with blood in autumn-time,
Who promises to stay until the Dawn.

To give a name, perpetuate a name,
And breathe upon the coals an infant's song…
Rejuvenate a cooling ember-flame.

Moss Agate

And thus the Grene Knyht sports with Arthur's band,
Transience meets immortality—
Sir Gawain strikes the blow, beheads the Man…

As I behead last summer's stiff-mown weeds
Bold-grown and proud—ruff-necked, haut, gaudy for
My fatal stroke. Rude act—rude play, perhaps—
But necessary (as I think)—green gore
To pay for Fall's regenerative lapse—
Yet from the crystal-sharded rime of snow
Dendritic aches to full contractions swell
Seeded by the frozen-garnet glow
That with my hasty sword-stroke, dying, fell—

Molecule upon molecule tissue-flesh
Rebuilds, rises into spring breezes fresh

Plantings

On the North side he planted irises—
Raw-barren tubers spearing eave-hung shade
Where firs had sheltered before Christmases.

In front, facing the West, toward the road,
She planted roses, pre-echoing frail
Petals drifting endlessly on grass,
On stone, on clotted clods along fence rails.

In back, to the East, we children had
Our six-foot lengths to grow our chosen seeds—
Mine, *Butterfly Wings*, light, fragmentary
Next to stolid sunflowers and invasive weeds.

But South, along the drive, as if wary
Of being caught, I kept *Nicotiana*
In its gallon pot…half rebel…half-sorry.

First Taste

It was my first taste of Idaho peach
Moments off the branch, redolent with heat
And cold co-mixed. I remember I reached
For the largest, yellow-red, scented sweet.

It struck, sharp, quick—a wasp-blade in my neck,
A burning pain that startled before it
Even began to hurt. A second's tick—
Then I screamed, a six-year-old's banshee-fit.

It smoothed, cold and numbing on tight, hot flesh,
Soft mud where the wasp had stung, soothed there by
My grandfather's coarse-now-gentle grip. Fresh
Ease eroded pain, calm replaced wild cries.

I now feared wasps—unseen, deceptive wisps.
I ate the peach—squashed, pulpy in my fist.

Wire-Art

And when the stones spin whispers—
Gentle fragment-colloquies—
Uttered along broad finger-
Tips—the solid flesh—the eyes—

Muscles whisper answers
Back—a twist—a fold—a curve—
That echoes in a silver whirl—
A gold-metallic word—

And join the stone—as Symbionts—
Enmeshed in matrix-mood—
And neither one—perhaps—is clear
Which stands as stone and which as blood

Trilobites
With Aunt Amy, Fossil-Hunting in Southern Utah, c. 1955

90,000,000 years add ponderous weight—
Another score (or more?)—insensate Time
Impenetrably dense, as surface freight
Accumulates—spread grain by grain, sands limn
Silicon exchange—life and stone mate,
Twine…, urged crystal-echoes form and mime
Rigid carapace, each fleshly state
Within—density and measured hardness climb—
Until—with wind and rain, with flame and ice—
Mortised coffin-joints expand—austere walls
Disintegrate—alluvium (contrite
Perhaps) compresses to prolong the game…

Then fragments into crumbled sandstone cauls
And cuff-link-mounted, lacquered trilobites.

FirstDreams

       …late night SummerDreams
green concrete patio-fresh
muffled in curving nylon folds—
flesh of dreams in dreams of flesh

blue-liquid-green-turquoise spotted
by etching light, swiveled and swirled
LightDream drawing instants to
eternities, revealing worlds

unfelt….
    Flutter-flicker eyes and
parched breath breathe blue-liquid-green—
fingers curve to touch to smooth taut
aching DreamLines in pools unseen

except in late-night hot-night SummerDreams
where blood ignites in swirled, half-known gleams

Love Sonet in Refracted Fragments
of Umber Light

honey-dark   curving   sweetly fold from
fold   into extended
possibility   haunting glimmer-glance

home told   crested shadows up and
down   until descended
dissipating   taunting shimmer-chance

anew   again   bows and bold-fold forms
field   against defended
weighting   daunting dimmer-dance

blue-white   under/over umber plover fans
fancied   through intended
probability   jaunty   simmer-stance

Something about the Curve of Lip

Something about the curve of lip   the fem-
inine   almost   or at the least the am-
biguity   that signals startle/shock   com-
pels attention and a farrowed brow—

or twist of fingertip   outreached and over-
reached crookhook/stiff celluloidal arc
to signify both trans-/port and -/for-
mation   embodied in geologic

greys—or worse and more   some turn of thought/em-
pulse fivedactyldrive-focus on the mas-

culine   not-with-knowing   beneath blueden-
im   cord/duroy   caught in shadows from the past

Without a newyork

without a newyork where to scrabble sour
anonymity of sweatbond streets   al-
-leyways that hunker darkness thru long-dour
casementbricks— —where to see   touch   taste ill-

-licits   where among stark panhard widestreet
brightlit immortal sunbaked nothinged bak-
-ersfields— —on low back-shelves   past rows of greet-
-ingcards   dietaids   slick porcelains   lurk

moments gasp-grasped in the storm   breath-choked-sigh
fragments   convertible-plymouth top-down-
-nude parked ill-legally beneath a vi-
-olated half-moon sun   in side-longing tones

of b/w glints   slickporous papered sub-
-stitutes for neverknown newyorks   poorchild

MISCELLANY
For Judi

The First Day Is of Spirit and of Mind

The first day is of Spirit and of Mind,
The slow unfolding of two growing seeds
And reaching tendrils that in time must bind
One to another, meet each for other's needs.

The second day becomes a time of deeds;
The tendrils thicken, strengthen, become arms
That, intertwining, form one life that feeds
On love—and in its joining receives no harms.

The third day—loneliness and wild alarms
As two united souls are pulled apart;
But in our hearts cold lonely feeling warms
As He sows sweetest joys 'mid sorrows tart.

The tendrils lengthen, stretch o'er myriad miles,
And waiting spirits share in timeless smiles.

...And Her Own Works

> "...And Her Own Works
> Praise Her In the Gates"
> —Proverbs 31:31

When we were two, through God's word joined as one,
Were sealed for Eternity in love,
It seemed the greatest blessings from above
Were in her eyes, her voice, for me alone;
   When we were three, I held my firstborn son,
And knew my wife a mother pure and sweet,
Saw unborn children kneeling near her feet
To learn of prayer, to love what God has done;
   When we become great multitudes, when none

Shall fail, but our belovèd children live
Eternally, and to our Father give
Deep love, their mother's glory shall be won;
    Then shall her children's eyes to her upraise,
And they with me shall sing her Godhood's praise.

Futility—Sonet to FF

I read the poems of a long-past age—
Rate florid diction, dull formality—
And wonder how—or if—I could engage
Their idioms in verse-normality....
That is, create a sonnet or an ode
That sounds and reads like modern, spoken lines,
That yet retains its rigid genre-code
To give it meaning—while remaining *mine!*

And then—in midst of worry and despair,
Engulfed by high-archaic *'twas* and *'twere*—
I think on clear blue eyes and flowing hair,
On sweetnesses surpassing fabled myrrh—
And recognize the vast futility—
To capture you escapes my poor ability.

We Flew—Sonet to FF

we flew last night in my so-vivid
dreams   flew   you and I
while other couples walked sly beaches
hand on hand   we

flew   the very touch of flesh to flesh
and earthen steps swept
airward   highbound   lightning wild
in cloudless skies

we flew   and fly   you and I   each time
you smile   you glance   you sigh
but then I knew   felt   saw   in dreams
what here lies metaphor

we flew   and fly
you and I

A Solitary Aubade—Sonet to FF

And I know she's sleeping, dance
on dance beneath snow plummets
feather-late— and now I know the cadence
of her breathing to the warmth of hammock-
sun-to-be when Day-brakes slow and don
sweet wavering of heat and hope and sweat—
and now she's gone—
smoothness, warmth, and breath of petals wet

with due-concern for what is past— and now
I wake alone and wish
it once again as once it was— and now
I wake alone and wish

Patience

At night, when daylight fails and sounds diminish
to a breath beyond mere nothingness…when lives
like light cast no more shadows but are replenished
by the shadow-death of sleep…when conscience-knives
lie blunted by the body's sharp fatigue
and hopes transform to gossamer in dreams—

then and then and then…the inner dig
begins. A buzz. A ring. A shallow stream

of non-poetic susurrations wrap
the pillowcase in wakefulness. Sleep
retires the field in defeat, trapped
by ceaseless sounds that, like spies, seep
by corners and can be vanquished only through
the voice and touch of one enduring You.

Butterflies

Our oldest son approaches his nineteenth year;
    Our youngest daughter stretches to fourteen—
    Those entrusted for our love and guidance
Have learned—are learning—to glide their single flights.
Our chosen task of parenting is muted,
    Our task of being peers and friends begun—
    We watch them spreading unknown glitter-wings,
And swallow loss, drink pangs of jealousy.
Our parents slowly grow to be ourselves;
    We are them as we saw them lives ago—
    We struggle into complex, rhythmic patterns
Of aging and increased duality.
And we complete the nervous, anxious round,
Retaining only fragments of shattered cocoons.

For Thy Sake

I spaded in the garden again today,
Adam being in the fields to husband wheat.
So I spaded in the garden, remembering
Eden: roses twining glossy ivy on
A smooth oak trunk, such massed perfumes
That I could scarcely stand. Or apricots
And peaches, gold and blush, bowing stiff-spined
Branches earthward. I needed merely look,
Or pluck and eat, or smell.
And tomorrow, I shall spade again, for now

the apricots, the peaches, and the rose
belong to me.

In the World

Apotheosis

"Sing pipes! and strain with song thy brazen throats,
Rumble deepest Bourdon, soft-breathe Flute,
Lest silence else the quivering air dilute
Or strangle into nothing lingered notes;
    "Be live! ye lifeless Diapason woods,
Vibrate with rushed bursts of pented air,
Lest resting hearts submit to grave despair
Or spirit-heights descend to muted moods;
    "Transcend the formal pattern—black on white—
Prepare the apotheosis of sound,
Release mind-soul in chains of earth-thought bound
To rise above benighted spheres of sight."

The notes combine, soft-fluid powers compel,
And me expand through meditation's swell.

On Singing *The Star-Spangled Banner* at a Missionary Farewell

We stood and sang (sixteen long years now past,
When you were still a child)...we stood and sang
Beneath the red, the white, the blue.
                            At last
The time had come for us to leave; we rang
The anthem to a battle's fevered clang
And cried our silent pain. For two far years
We would sing mutely, sing against the pang
Of loneliness. We learned to touch new fears,

To transmute sorrows into whispered cheers,
To speak of Christ and witness lives new-born,
To share our lives and grow through loves and tears—
For two short fleeting years—until the thorn
Of time came fully round. We stood to raise
The anthem once again in welling praise.

Malibu Fires
Early Morning, 3 November 1993

4 AM—and I startle awake at the sound
of an Anchor repeating 'Pepperdine!'—and slap-
ping glasses to bridge of nose I peer around
the sofa's arm at the TV screen, at snap-
ping static and embers igniting eucalyptus;
and 'The school is threatened,' the unbodied voice declaims,
'The fire is raging out of control! Worse
than the worst imaginings!' and glitter flames
beyond two figures wrapped in ash and smoke,
and two more struggle with canvas hoses…snakes
coiled through mustard air that stings and chokes
and burns, and I push my glasses up, hand shak-
ing heart thrusting lobes against lungs that burst
in panic at dreaming bad, worse,…and worst.

ER 8/2/84, 4:15 PM

I saw fear in his eyes...and death
as he lay on the shrunken grey bed
while buzzes and bleeps monitored
beat and breath. The room hung curtained
in white with jagged stripes of blue
and red—faint EKG tapes pulled-
tugged a body worn in fight.
He lay ashen, shrunken—motion-
less except his eyes, puppy's eyes

surveying their new home with pan-
ic, manic, red-eyed fear.
I entered, touched a forearm flaccid,

Looked into my father's eyes and saw
his father—looked…and saw myself.

Odyssey I
From the Back of Time and Form [Cento]

Children are dumb to say how hot the day is,
No sleep. The sultriness pervades the air
To force the pace and never to be still—
Our little tantrum, flushed and misery-hollow.

Cedar and jagged fir—Earth place—
Nothing, not even fear of punishment
(The flat place of sorrow here)
Opening like a marigold,

Crossing the street.
Each day the time grows less, the hours
Now as I was young and easy under the apple boughs
Time that is moved by little fidget wheels

On broad hills, the broken
backs of mountains.

Odyssey II
Telemachus Speaks [Cento]

"Nature is evil," Midas said,
Brushing back the curls from your famous brow,
The garland briefer than a girl's
Sometimes under the night
Along the river

My father and I play checkers
I want to belong to the third sex—
The first answer was incorrect.

Do we dare, now, to open our eyes.
Odysseus has come home, to the gully farm,
Back into life, back to the gods—
He slept like a rock, or a man that's dead.
Go and find *work*
Till human voices wake us, and we drown.

BIBLIOGRAPHY

Andrus, Hyrum L. *God, Man, and the Universe. Volume I: Foundations of the Millennial Kingdom of Christ.* Salt Lake City UT: Bookcraft, 1968.

Barber, Richard. *King Arthur: Hero and Legend.* 3 ed. Suffolk, England: Boydell, 1986.

Barrett, Ivan J. *Joseph Smith and the Restoration: A History of the LDS Church to 1846.* 1967. Rev. ed. Provo UT: Brigham Young University Press, 1973.

Buxton, John. *Elizabethan Taste.* London and New York: Macmillan/St. Martin's, 1966.

Cannon, George Q. *The Life of Joseph Smith, the Prophet.* Salt Lake City UT: Juvenile Instructor Office, 1888.

Falco, Raphael. *Conceived Presences: Literary Genealogy in Renaissance England.* Amherst MA: University of Massachusetts Press, 1994. 148. Citing Erwin Panofsky.

Gibbons, Francis M. *Joseph Smith: Martyr, Prophet of God.* Salt Lake City UT: Deseret Book Company, 1977.

Goodrich, Peter, ed. *The Romance of Merlin.* New York: Garland, 1990.

Hooker, Jeremy. *David Jones: An Exploratory Study of the Writings.* London: Enitharmon Press, 1975.

Lacy, Norris J., and Geoffrey Ashe. *The Arthurian Handbook.* New York: Garland, 1988.

Lewis, C. S., and Charles Williams. *The Arthurian Torso. 1948.* One-Volume edition. Grand Rapids MI: William B. Eerdmanns, 1974.

Matthias, John, ed. *Introducing David Jones: A Selection of His Writings, with a preface by Stephen Spender.* London: Faber and Faber, 1980.

Nibley, Hugh. *Temple and Cosmos: Beyond This Ignorant Present.* Edited by Don E. Norton. Salt Lake City UT: Deseret Book Company, and Provo UT: Foundation for Ancient Research and Mormon Studies, 1992.

Pratt, Parley P. *Key to the Science of Theology: Designed as an Introduction to the First Principles of Spiritual Philosophy, Religion, Law and Government, as Delivered by the Ancients, and as Restored in This Age, for the Final Development of Universal Peace, Truth and Knowledge.* 1853. 4th Edition. Salt Lake City UT: Deseret News Company, 1883.

Smith, Joseph Fielding, comp. *Teachings of the Prophet Joseph Smith.* 1938. Salt Lake City UT: Deseret Book Company, 1974.

Smith, Lucy Mack. *History of Joseph Smith, By His Mother, Lucy Mack Smith.* Notes and Comments by Preston Nibley. Salt Lake City: Bookcraft, 1958.

Widtsoe, John A.. *A Rational Theology As Taught by the Church of Jesus Christ of Latter-day Saints.* Salt Lake City UT: General Boards of the Mutual Improvement Associations, 1915; 3rd edition 1932.

Wilhelm, James J. *The Romance of Arthur: An Anthology of Medieval Texts in Translation.* New, Expanded Edition. New York: Garland, 1994.

Williams, Charles. *Taliessin through Logres/The Region of the Summer Stars.* 1938, 1944. One-volume edition. Grand Rapids MI: William B. Eerdman's, 1974.

Woodruff, Wilford. *Leaves from My Journal, Third Book of the Faith-Promoting Series, Designed for the Instruction and Encouragement of Young Latter-Day Saints.* 2nd Edition. Salt Lake City UT: Juvenile Instructor Office, 1882.

Yates, Frances A. *The Art of Memory.* Chicago: University of Chicago Press, 1966.

TITLE INDEX

1,000,000, 42
13 Vultures, 135
African Violets, 33
After Diagnosis, 50
After First Blooding, 56
After Spring Rain, 31
Air, 91
Alchemy, 29
Amnesia, 19
Anamnesis, 61
"…And Her Own Works Praise Her in the Gates," 144
And Yet the Stones Endure, 82
Apotheosis, 148
Arthur and Guinevere, 70
Arthur and the Head of Bran, 68
Arthur and the Mountains, 74
Arthur and the Serpents, 71
Arthur Blesses a Faithful Knight, 71
Arthur's Great Hall, 75
Arthur's Knight Returns the Blessing, 78
Aurora Borealis, 37
Author's Afterword: What in the World—Any World!—Is This Fellow Up To?, 119
Because the Father, 48
Because Your Sister, 44
Before the Throwing, 20

Besieged, 60
Beyond the Plains, 25
Birth, 21
Blackbird Fall, 135
Blood Rite, 114
Bluebottle Flies, 35
Bruce and the Cow, 23
Butterflies, 147
Children's Merry-Go-Round, The, 22
Console, 112
Cormorant, 134
Countdown—Thirteen Hours Gone…Thirty-Five to Go, 103
Creation, 88
Creekrock, 111
Cutting the Tree, 30
Dance of the Post-Millennial Hours, 104
Darkness in the Light, 55
"Death, Be Not Proud," 59
Death on a Dirt-Road Highway, 34
Dedication: Taliesin to Brother Prayer, 64
Desiccated Flame, 106
Drive-In, 40
Eagle, 109
Earthquake, 38
Ecstasy of S. Teresa di Avila, The, 60
Edmund Homer's Bucksaw, 43
Elegy, 58
Elementals, 87
Envoi: Return to the Homestead, 62
Envoi: Taliesin's Testament, 83
ER 8/2/84, 4:51 pm, 149
Exotica—Elemental Sonet, 126
Falling Water, 95
Father's Day, 32
Fence Posts…And Thus the Past Proceeds, 58
Fifth Movement…And Final, 105

First Day is of Spirit and of Mind, The, 144
First Job, 46
First Snowfalls, 31
First Taste, 138
FirstDreams, 139
Fishing with Cousin Ray, 30
Fog, Like Snow, 95
For Thy Sake, 147
Foreword: A Banquet of Sonets, 124
From the Porch [I], 21
From the Porch [II], 39
Futility, 145
Gardening Taken as an Act of Compassionate Service, 54
Glimpses, 129
GodFinger, 108
Grail, The, 70
Grampa Collings, 24
Grandmother Collings's Church-House in Jerome, 25
Greenery, 110
Gwyn Tour, 99
Hæmatite, 127
Hailstones, 33
Harvest Crows, 134
Hombres, Mexico, 93
Hummingbird, 132
I Have Set My Feet, 81
In a Distant Other-When, 59
In Elba the Chapel was Light, 26
In the Old House on the Farm, 20
In Therapy Today, 52
Introduction: Why 'Sonets'?, 9
It…A Suspicion and an Apprehension, 47
J. Roy Eames' General Store, 28
Jigsaw Puzzles, 131
Just Like Beethoven, 49
Last Night I Dreamed of Empty Shelves, 51

LiveOak, 107
Love Sonet in Refracted Fragments of Umber Light, 140
Lying Hand-Crossed in Her Satin Box, 56
Magdalene, 45
Magpie, 132
Malibu Fires, 149
Mason Jars, 36
Minotaur [II], 101
Mirror Lake, 40
MoonMasks, 89
Mosquitoes, 35
Moss Agate, 136
Mountain Hike, 130
Music of the Spheres, 116
My Eyes Stayed Closed, 51
Naked on Its Branch the Shadow Stands, 93
Nellie, Outside the House, Jerome ID, 1935, 23
Night, 115
Nobbled as an Eagle's Claw, 48
NY/LA Any Moment/Any Day, 102
Odyssey I: From the Back of Time and Form, 150
Odyssey II: Telemachus Speaks, 150
On a Display of Swordsmanship, 113
On First Acquaintance with an Insulin Syringe, 53
On Poetry as a Façade Behind Which the Essence Lurks, 13
On Seeing Photographs of My Grandfather in His Middle-Age, 129
On Seeing the Unretouched Original…, 103
On Singing The Star-Spangled Banner at a Missionary Farewell, 148
On Speaking a Child's Blessing in November, 136
On Stress, 14
Operation in a Country Church, 26
Orion, 41
Passing of the Old Guard, The, 28
Patience, 146

Peach Jam, 41
Plantings, 137
Predator, 113
Quasimodo from the Cathedral's Pinnacle, 131
Rain, 98
Relay Race, 37
Remembering the Flight of Wingless Birds, 55
SandStone, 96
Scars, 27
Seashallows, 97
Second Row Behind the Deacons, Side Aisle, 34
Silently, as with a Blade-Edge…, 116
Sitting on a Rock to Watch the Dawn, 57
Sleeping in the Basement, 36
Sleeping Out, 43
Slides, 46
Snowdrops, 44
Solitary Aubade, A, 146
Solstice-Born, The, 67
Some Portraits of the Poet…, 52
Something about the Curve of Lip, 140
Sonata Contorta, 107
Sonnet, 19
Sparkle, 42
Sputnik, 32
Stalker's Sonet, A, 100
Stringing Buttons, 22
Summer, 1953, 27
Swallows, 133
Taliesin and Arthur's Majesty, 72
Taliesin and the Kings, 69
Taliesin and the Lamb, 76
Taliesin and the Questions, 73
Taliesin at the Grave of Arthur, 77
Taliesin Bemoans His Loss of Words, 76
Taliesin Broods on the Order of Succession…, 80

Taliesin Considers Excalibur, 71
Taliesin Contemplates the Vanity of His Works, 78
Taliesin Dreams of Seagulls, 79
Taliesin Mourns for the Pelicans, 80
Taliesin Overlooks the Ruins of Camelot, 77
Taliesin Reacts to Arthur's Revelation, 75
Taliesin Recounts the Wound to Arthur's Leg, 67
Taliesin to Autumn, 82
Taliesin to His Harp, 65
Taliesin to His Solemn Self, in His Old Age, 81
Taliesin to Light, 66
Taliesin to the Stones, 68
Taliesin Witnesses the Commission to the Table, 74
Taliesin Writes an Elegy for a Swallow, 79
Taliesin's Vision of the Wondrous Pillars…, 72
Thistles, 98
Tinnitus, 128
Tinnitus—At the Organ, 128
To Eat a Peach, 45
To the Wilds, 61
Tornado, 92
Trilobites, 139
Twister, 39
Vacant Lots, 38
Voice from the Dust, 49
Volcano, 90
We Flew, 145
What Might Follow Fire, 50
When the Pipes Blew, 54
Where the White Crow Flies, 133
Why Epyllion in Anamnesis?, 13
Why Was the Path to the Outhouse So Long?, 29
Wire-Art, 138
Without a NewYork, 141

ABOUT THE AUTHOR

MICHAEL R. COLLINGS is an Emeritus Professor of English at Seaver College, Pepperdine University, where he directed the Creative Writing Program for over two decades. He has published multiple volumes of poetry, novels, short fiction, and scholarly studies of such contemporary writers as Stephen King, Orson Scott Card, Dean R. Koontz, and Piers Anthony. Recent works include *The Art and Craft of Poetry*; *In the Void: Poems of Science Fiction, Myth and Fantasy, and Horror*; *Matrix: Growing Up West—Autobiographical Poems*; and a Book of Mormon epic, *The Nephiad*.

His fiction, also published through Wildside, includes: *The House Beyond the Hill: A Novel of Fear*; *Wordsmith, Volume One: The Thousand Eyes of Flame* and *Wordsmith, Volume Two: The Veil of Heaven*; *Singer of Lies*; *Wer Means Man, and Other Tales of Wonder and Terror*; *Three Tales of Omne: A Companion to* Wordsmith; and *The Slab,* the story of a haunted tract house in Southern California…that consumes people.

He is now retired and lives in his native state of Idaho.

www.ingramcontent.com/pod-product-compliance
Lightning Source LLC
LaVergne TN
LVHW041625070426
835507LV00008B/455